TOP HITS OF 2020

Front cover ukulele photo courtesy of Flight Instruments

ISBN 978-1-70511-121-5

HAL•LEONARD®

For all works contained herein:
Unauthorized copying, arranging, adapting, recording, Internet posting, public performance,
or other distribution of the music in this publication is an infringement of copyright.
Infringers are liable under the law.

Visit Hal Leonard Online at
www.halleonard.com

Contact us:
Hal Leonard
7777 West Bluemound Road
Milwaukee, WI 53213
Email: info@halleonard.com

In Europe, contact:
Hal Leonard Europe Limited
42 Wigmore Street
Marylebone, London, W1U 2RN
Email: info@halleonardeurope.com

In Australia, contact:
Hal Leonard Australia Pty. Ltd.
4 Lentara Court
Cheltenham, Victoria, 3192 Australia
Email: info@halleonard.com.au

Be Kind

Words and Music by Ashley Frangipane, Marshmello, Amy Allen, Gian Stone and Freddy Wexler

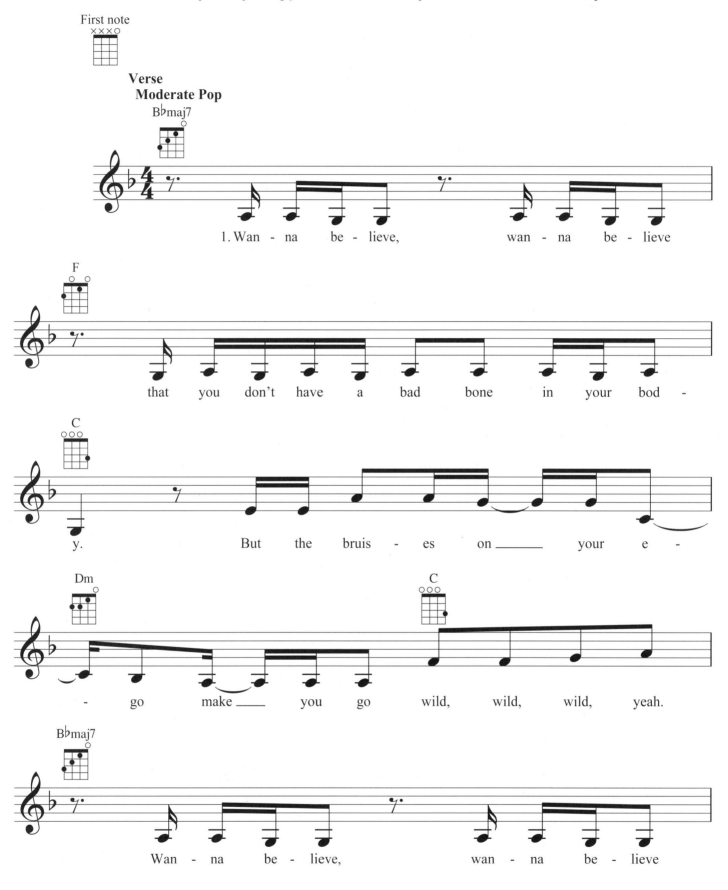

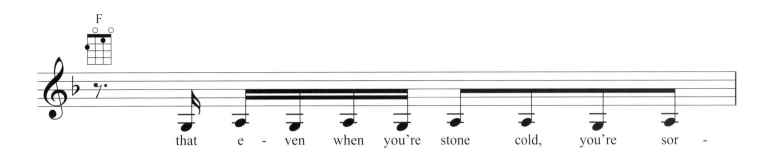

that e - ven when you're stone cold, you're sor -

ry. Tell me why you got - ta be ___ so out ___ of your mind, ___ yeah.

𝄋 Pre-Chorus

I know you're chok - ing on ___ your fears,

al - read - y told you I'm right here.

I will stay by your side ev - er - y night. I don't know why you

Chorus

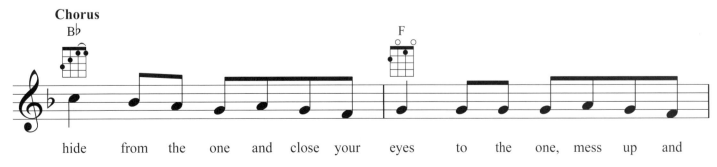

hide from the one and close your eyes to the one, mess up and

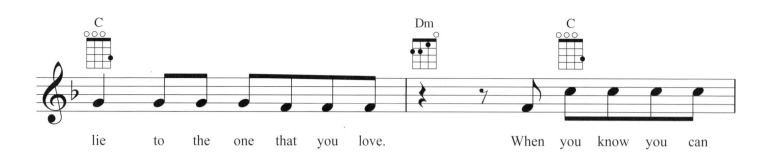

lie   to   the   one   that   you   love.   When   you   know   you   can

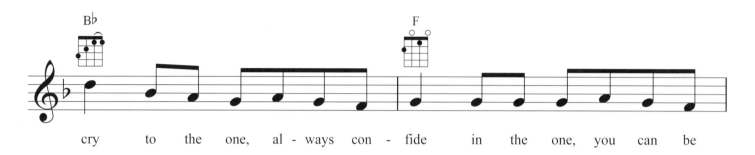

cry   to   the   one,   al - ways con - fide in   the   one,   you   can   be

To Coda ⊕

kind   to   the   one   that   you   love.   Ah. _____

Verse

N.C.

2. I   know   you   need,   I   know   you   need

the   up - per hand,   e - ven when   we   aren't   fight -

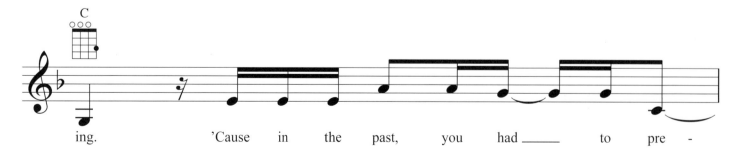

ing.   'Cause   in   the   past,   you   had _____ to   pre -

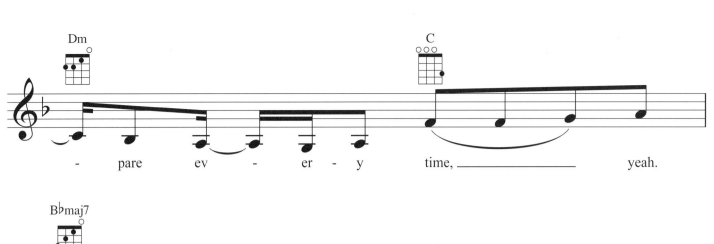

-pare ev - er - y time, _____ yeah.

Don't wan - na leave, don't wan - na leave,

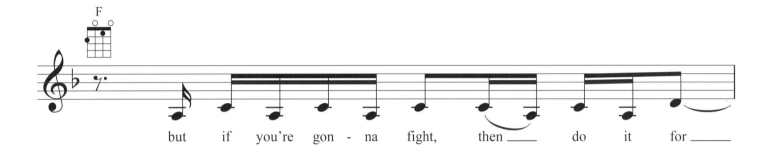

but if you're gon - na fight, then ___ do it for ___

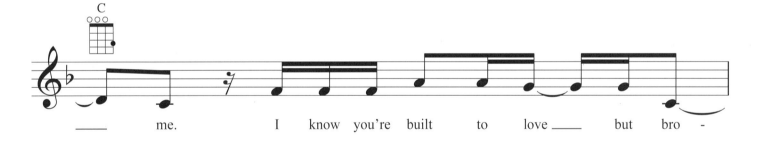

___ me. I know you're built to love ___ but bro -

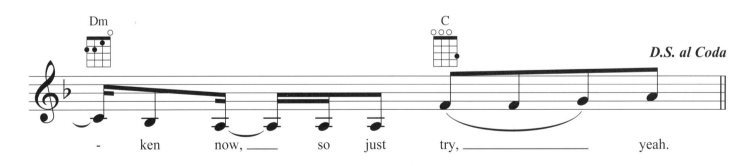

D.S. al Coda

- ken now, ___ so just try, _____ yeah.

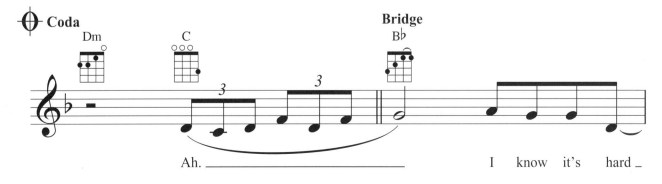

Ah. _____ I know it's hard _

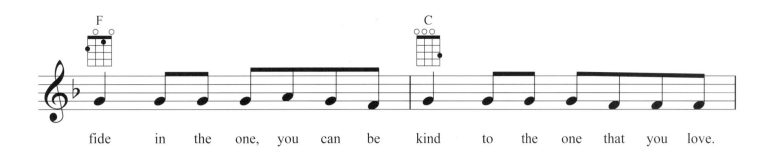

fide in the one, you can be kind to the one that you love.

Outro

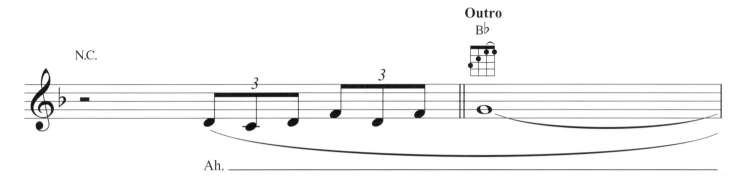

Ah. _____

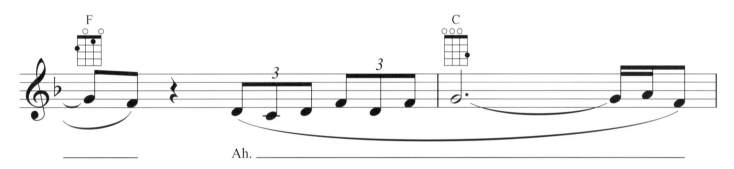

_____ Ah. _____

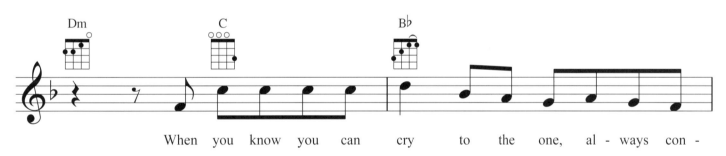

When you know you can cry to the one, al - ways con -

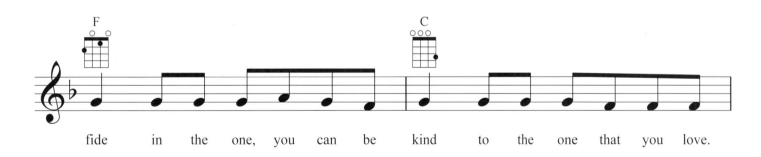

fide in the one, you can be kind to the one that you love.

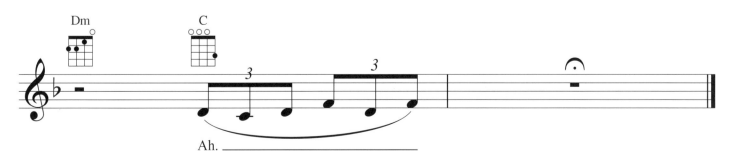

Ah. _____

Before You Go

Words and Music by Lewis Capaldi, Benjamin Kohn, Peter Kelleher, Thomas Barnes and Philip Plested

1. I fell by the way - side, _____ like ev - 'ry - one else.
2. Was nev - er the right time _____ when - ev - er you called.

"I hate you, I hate you, I hate you," but I was just kid - ding my - self.
Went lit - tle by lit - tle by lit - tle, un - til there was noth - ing at all.

Our ev - er - y mo - ment I start to re - place, _____
Our ev - er - y mo - ment I start to re - play, _____

_____ 'cause now that they're gone, all I hear are the words that I need - ed to say.
_____ but all I can think a - bout _____ is see - ing that look on your face.

Pre-Chorus

When you hurt un - der the sur - face, like trou - bled

wa - ter run - ning cold, _____ well, time can heal, but this won't. _

Chorus

So, be - fore you

go, was there some - thing I could -'ve said to make your

heart beat bet - ter? If on - ly I'd have known you had a

storm to weath - er. So, be - fore you go,

was there some - thing I could -'ve said to make it all stop hurt - ing? It

9

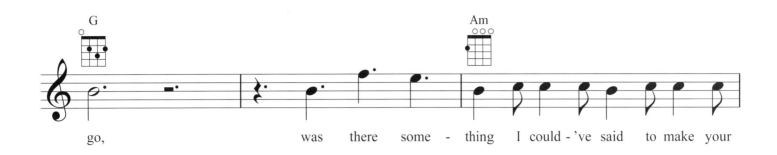

go,   was there some - thing I could - 've said to make your

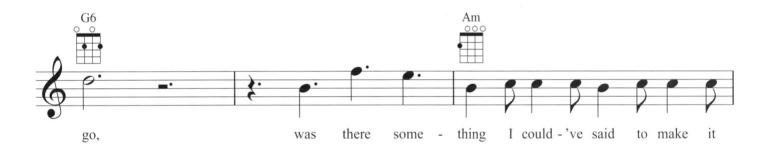

heart beat bet - ter? If on - ly I'd have known you had a

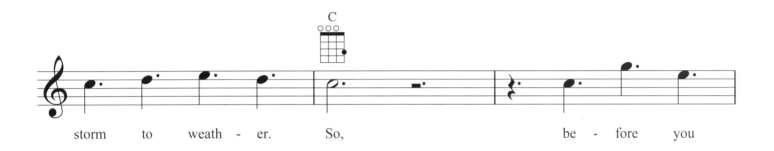

storm to weath - er. So,   be - fore you

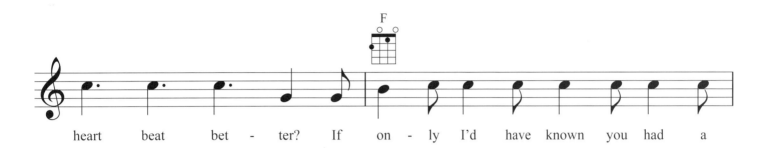

go,   was there some - thing I could - 've said to make it

all stop hurt - ing? It kills me how your mind can make you

feel so worth - less. So,   be-fore you go...

Better Days

Words and Music by Ryan Tedder, Brent Kutzle and John Nathaniel

First note

Chorus
Moderately

Oh, I know that there'll be bet - ter days. __

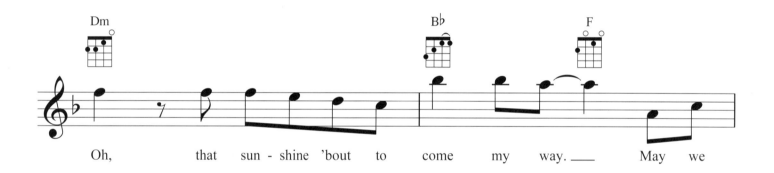

Oh, that sun - shine 'bout to come my way. __ May we

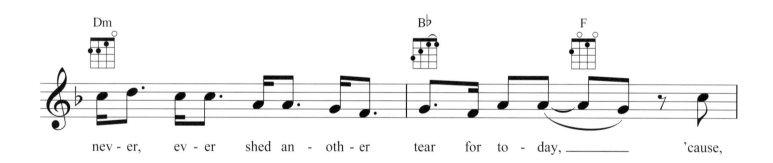

nev - er, ev - er shed an - oth - er tear for to - day, _____ 'cause,

To Coda

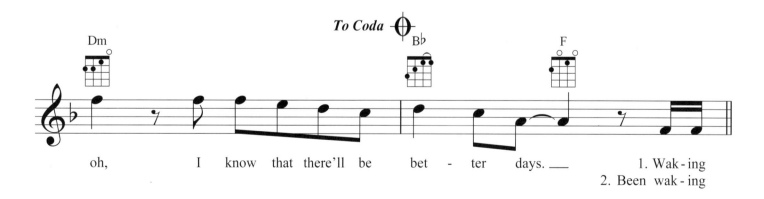

oh, I know that there'll be bet - ter days. __

1. Wak - ing
2. Been wak - ing

Verse

up in Cal - i - for - nia, ___ but these clouds, they won't go a - way. ___ Ev - 'ry
up ___ to a new year; ___ got the past a mil - lion miles a - way. ___ I've been wak - ing

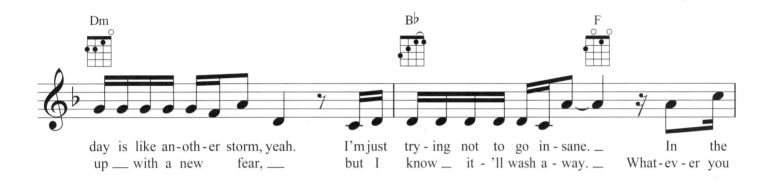

day is like an - oth - er storm, yeah. I'm just try - ing not to go in - sane. ___ In the
up ___ with a new fear, ___ but I know ___ it - 'll wash a - way. ___ What - ev - er you

cit - y shin - ing so bright, so man - y dark nights, so man - y dark days. But an - y - time I
do, don't wor - ry 'bout me. I'm think - ing 'bout you, don't wor - ry 'bout us. 'Cause in the

2nd time,
D.C. al Coda

feel the par - a - noi - a, _____ I close my eyes and I pray.
morn - ing, ev - 'ry - thing can change, _ yeah, and time will tell you it does.

Coda   **Bridge**

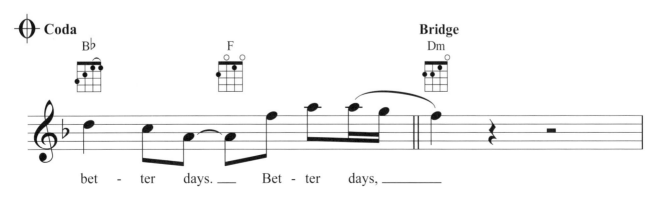

bet - ter days. ___ Bet - ter days, _____

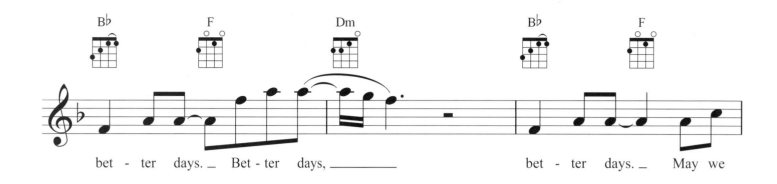

bet - ter days. _ Bet - ter days, _____ bet - ter days. _ May we

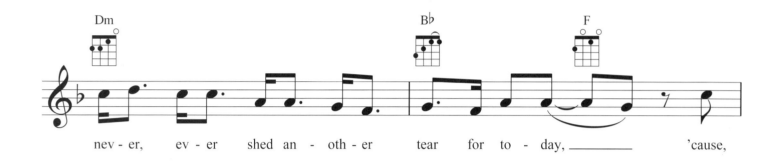

nev - er, ev - er shed an - oth - er tear for to - day, _____ 'cause,

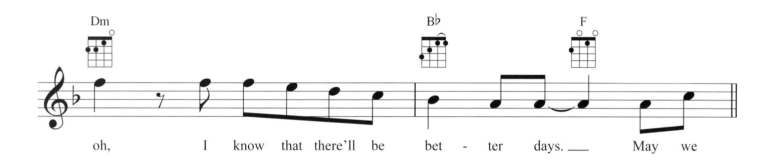

oh, I know that there'll be bet - ter days. ___ May we

Outro

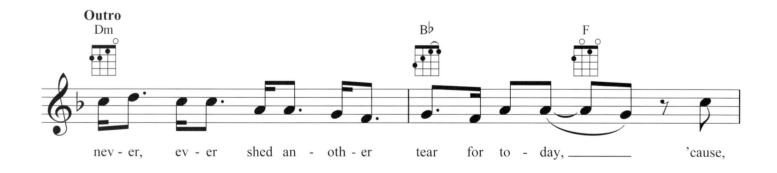

nev - er, ev - er shed an - oth - er tear for to - day, _____ 'cause,

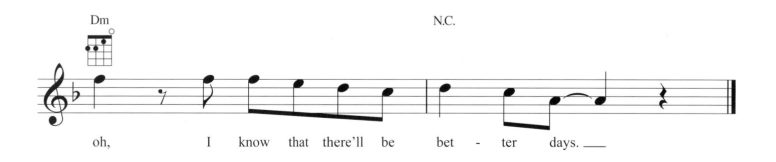

oh, I know that there'll be bet - ter days. ___

Adore You

Words and Music by Harry Styles, Thomas Hull, Tyler Johnson and Amy Allen

First note

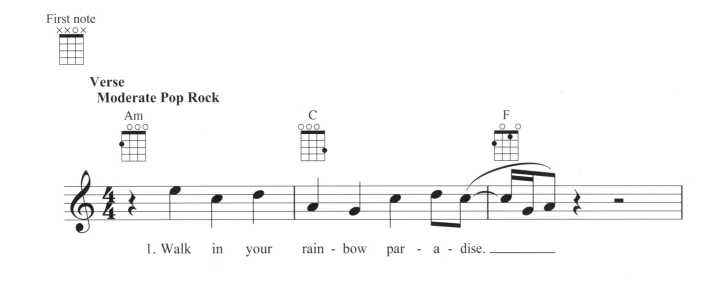

Verse
Moderate Pop Rock

1. Walk in your rain - bow par - a - dise. _____

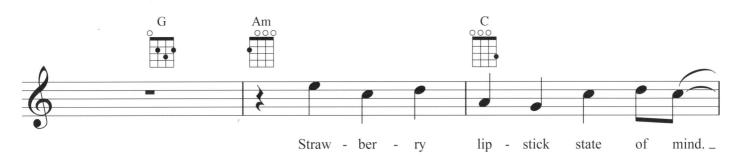

Straw - ber - ry lip - stick state of mind. _

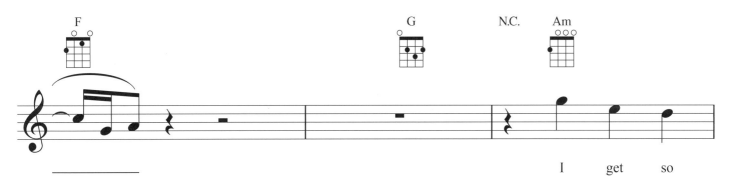

I get so

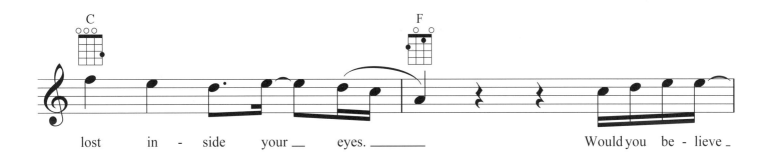

lost in - side your __ eyes. _____   Would you be - lieve _

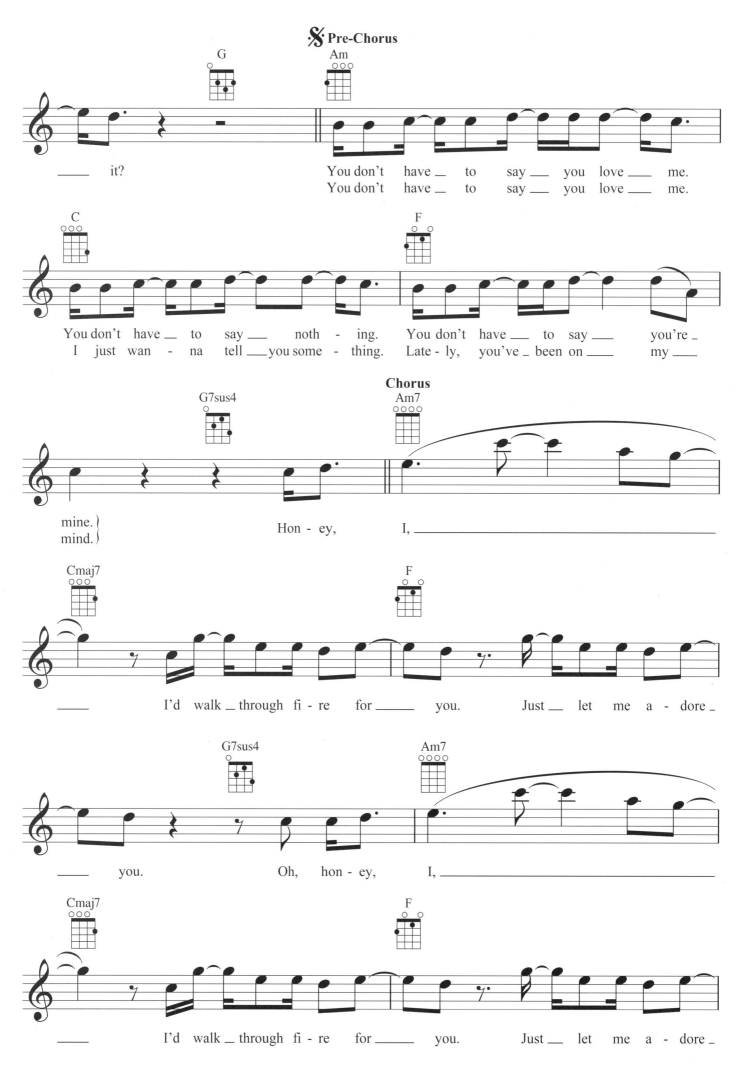

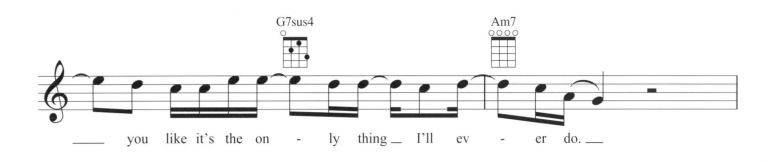

_____ you like it's the on - ly thing _ I'll ev - er do. __

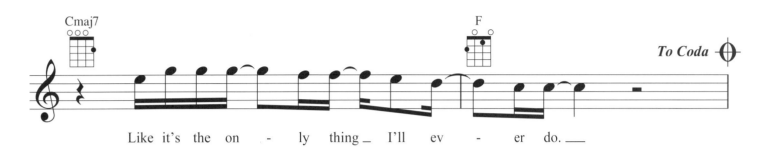

To Coda ⊕

Like it's the on - ly thing _ I'll ev - er do. ___

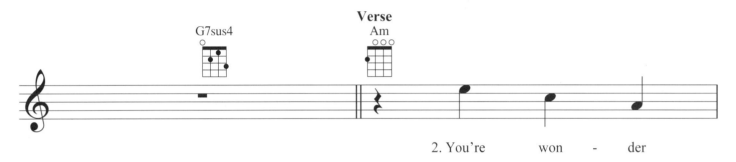

Verse

2. You're won - der

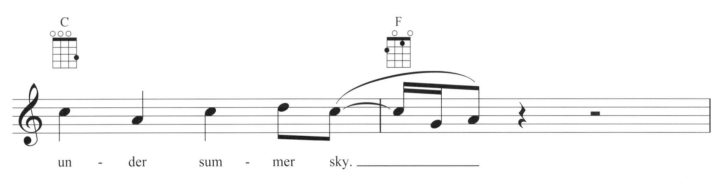

un - der sum - mer sky. _____

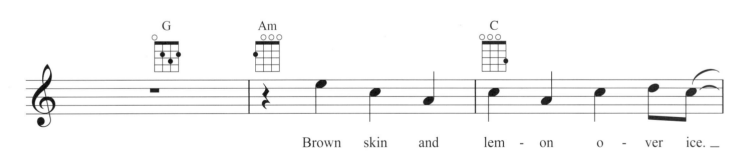

Brown skin and lem - on o - ver ice. _

D.S. al Coda

_____ Would you be - lieve ___ it?

Cardigan

Words and Music by Taylor Swift and Aaron Dessner

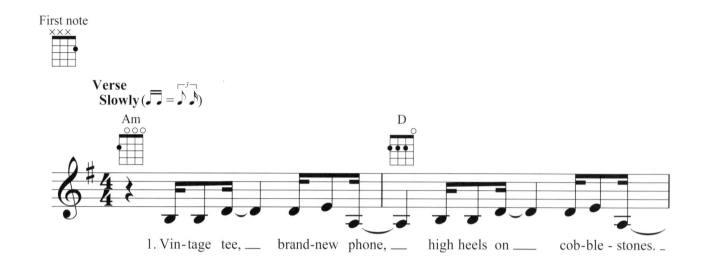

1. Vin-tage tee, __ brand-new phone, __ high heels on __ cob-ble - stones. __

__ When you are young, they as - sume you know noth - ing.

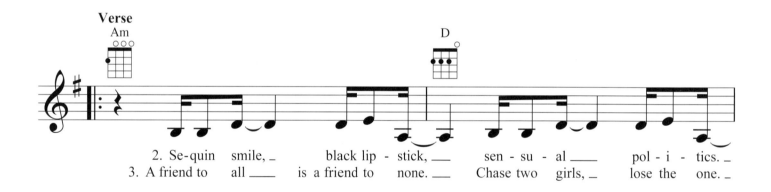

2. Se-quin smile, __ black lip - stick, __ sen-su - al __ pol - i - tics. __
3. A friend to all __ is a friend to none. __ Chase two girls, __ lose the one. __

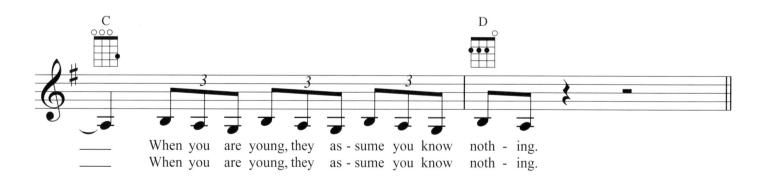

__ When you are young, they as - sume you know noth - ing.
__ When you are young, they as - sume you know noth - ing.

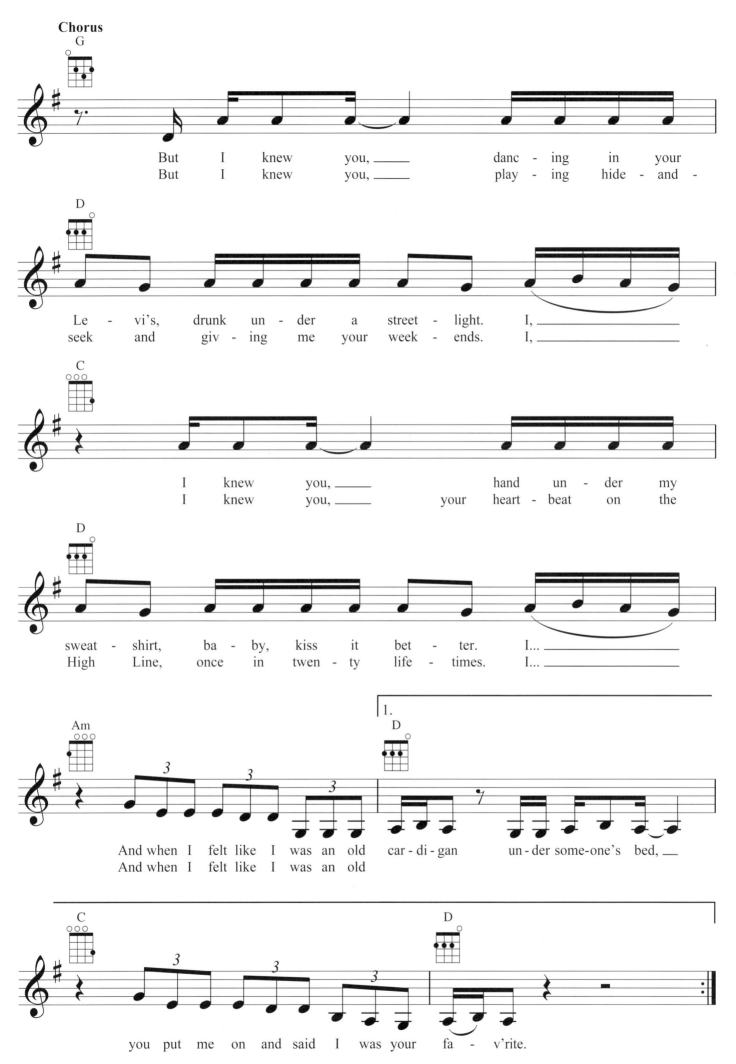

Chorus

But I knew you,＿＿ danc - ing in your
But I knew you,＿＿ play - ing hide - and -

Le - vi's, drunk un - der a street - light. I,＿＿＿＿＿＿
seek and giv - ing me your week - ends. I,＿＿＿＿＿＿

I knew you,＿＿ hand un - der my
I knew you,＿＿ your heart - beat on the

sweat - shirt, ba - by, kiss it bet - ter. I...＿＿＿＿＿
High Line, once in twen - ty life - times. I...＿＿＿＿＿

And when I felt like I was an old car - di - gan un - der some-one's bed,＿
And when I felt like I was an old

you put me on and said I was your fa - v'rite.

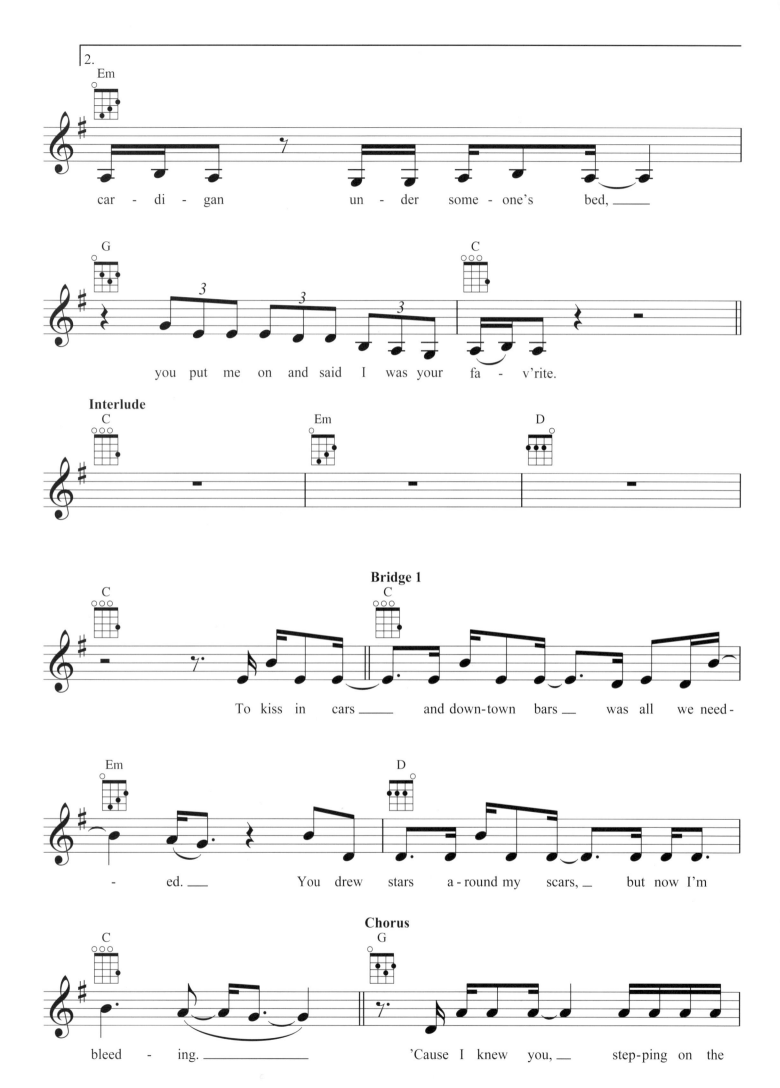

Interlude

Bridge 1

Chorus

last train, marked me like a blood - stain. I, _____

I knew you, _____ tried to change the

end - ing, Pe - ter los - ing Wen - dy. I, _____

I knew you, _ leav-ing like a fa - ther, run-ning like wa - ter. I... _

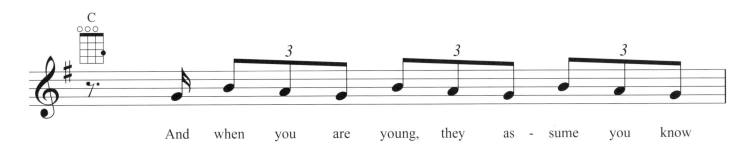

And when you are young, they as - sume you know

Bridge 2

noth - ing. But I knew you'd lin - ger like a tat-too kiss. _ I knew you'd haunt _

_____ all of _____ my "what ifs." _____ The smell of smoke _

_____ would hang a - round this long _____ 'cause I knew ev -

- 'ry - thing when I was young. _ I knew I'd curse _

_____ you for the long - est time, _____ chas - ing shad -

- ows in the gro - c'ry line. _____ I knew you'd miss _

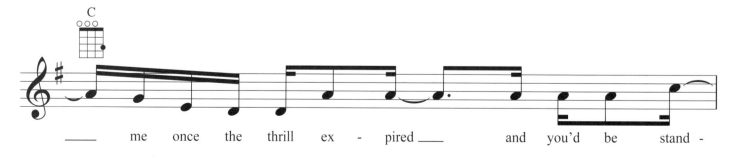

_____ me once the thrill ex - pired _____ and you'd be stand -

- ing in my front porch light. ___ And I knew you'd come back ___

___ to me, you'd come back ___ to me. And you'd come back ___

___ to me, and you'd come back. ___

Outro

And when I felt like I was an old

car - di - gan un - der some - one's bed, _____

you put me on and said I was your fa - v'rite.

I Dare You

Words and Music by Benjamin West, Jeffrey Gitelman,
Natalie Hemby, Laura Veltz and Jesse Shatkin

First note

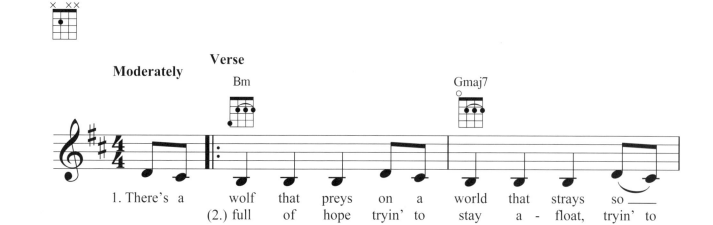

Verse

Moderately

1. There's a wolf that preys on a world that strays so ___
(2.) full of hope tryin' to stay a - float, tryin' to

far from the gar - den. And just like your ___ own, ev - 'ry
save one an - oth - er. Peo - ple let you ___ drown 'cause they

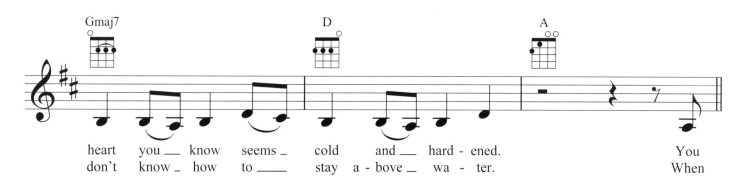

heart you ___ know seems ___ cold and ___ hard - ened. You
don't know ___ how to ___ stay a - bove ___ wa - ter. When

Pre-Chorus

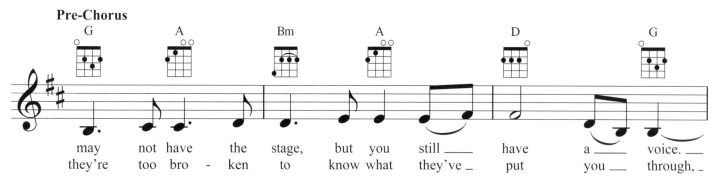

may not have the stage, but you still ___ have a ___ voice. ___
they're too bro - ken to know what they've ___ put you ___ through, ___

You may not have the strength, but if you ___
do the on-ly thing that you'd want ___

Chorus

have a ___ choice, ___
done to ___ you. ___ Oh, ___ I

dare you to love. ___ Oh, ___

I dare you to love. ___

E-ven if you're hurt and you can on-ly ___ see the worst.

E-ven if you think it's not e-nough. Oh, ___ I

dare   you   to   love. ____

2. We're   all   dare   you   to   love. _

Interlude

Just   dare   you   to   love, _

oh. _____

You

Pre-Chorus

may   not   have   the   stage,   but you   still __ have   a __ voice. ___

You

may   not   have   the   strength,   but   if   you __   have   a   choice, ___

Chorus
I dare you to love. ___

E-ven if you can't, _ no. ___ I dare you to love, ___

___ oh. E-ven if you're hurt and you can on-ly ___ see the worst.

E-ven if you think it's not e-nough. Oh, ___ I, I

Outro
dare you. I dare you. ___

Oh, ___ I, I dare you to love. ___

I'm Ready

Words and Music by Sam Smith, Demitria Lovato, Savan Kotecha, Anders Peter Svensson and Ilya Salmanzadeh

Verse

Male: 1. It's a cold night in my bed in the heat of the summer.

Female: 2. It's a hot night in my head in the chill of the winter.

I've been wait - ing pa - tient - ly for a beau - ti - ful lov - er. He's not a

I've been look - ing hard for a lov - er dis - guised as a sin - ner. Not a

* Female sings 2nd time 8vb.

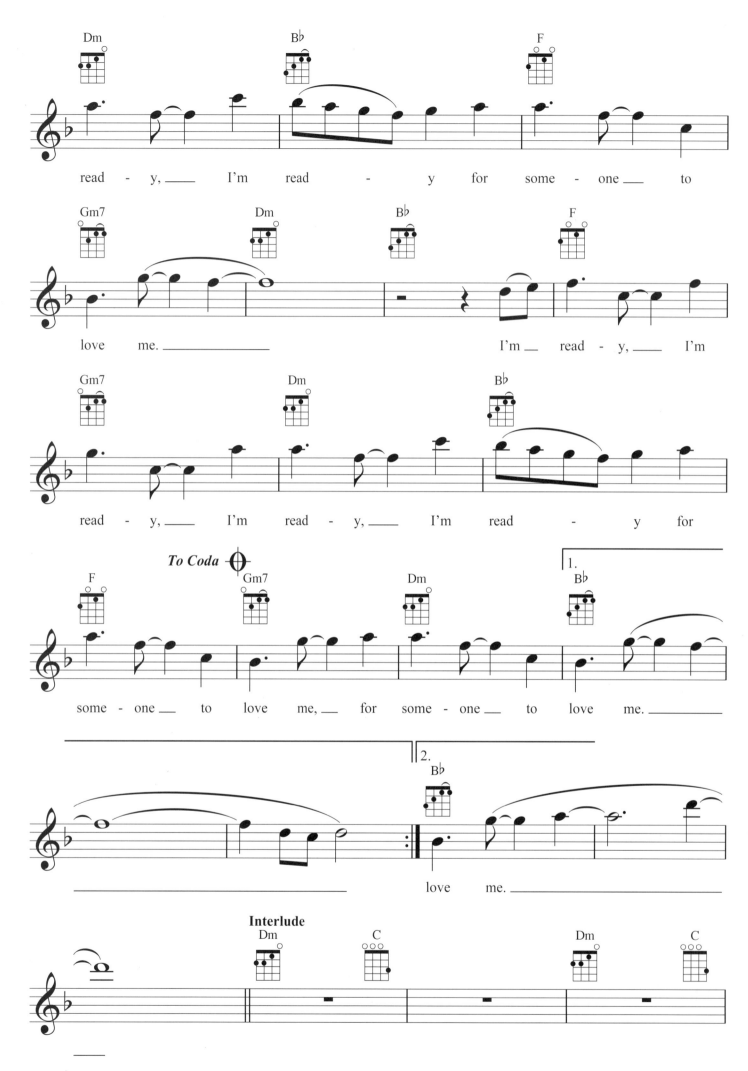

read - y, _____ I'm read - y for some - one _____ to

love me. _____ I'm _____ read - y, _____ I'm

read - y, _____ I'm read - y, _____ I'm read - y for

some - one _____ to love me, _____ for some - one _____ to love me. _____

love me. _____

In Your Eyes

Words and Music by Abel Tesfaye, Max Martin, Oscar Holter and Ahmad Balshe

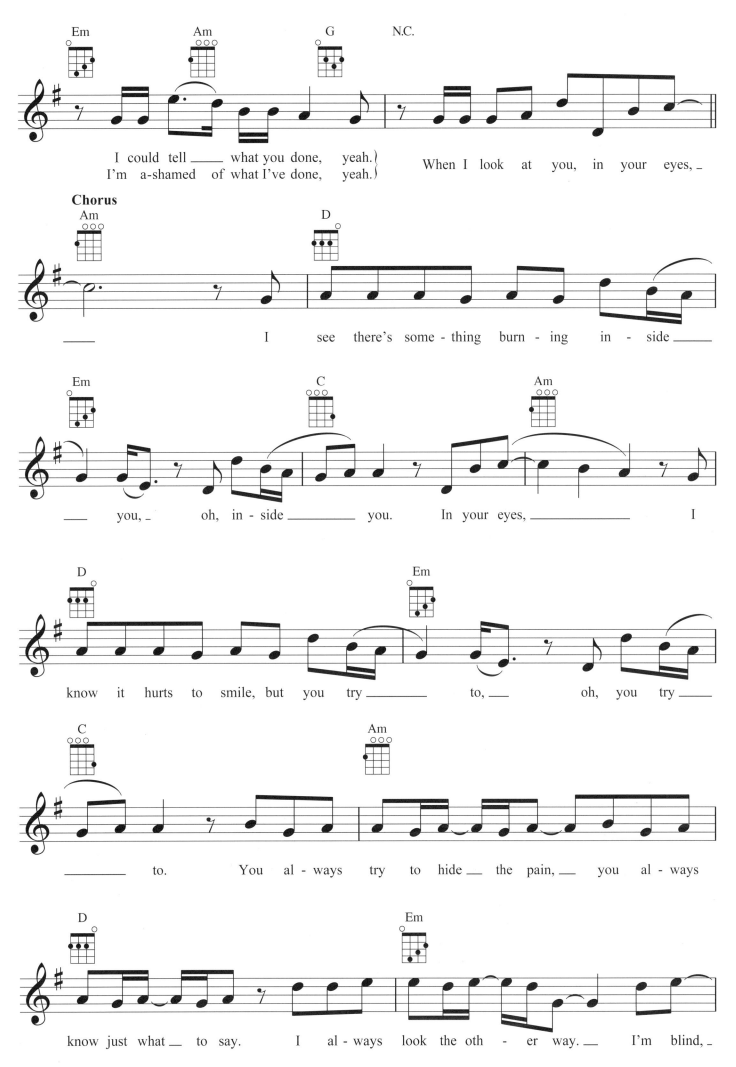

Chorus

look the oth - er way. ___ I'm blind, ___ I'm blind. ___ In your eyes, ___

___ you lie, but I don't let it de - fine ___

___ you, ___ oh, de - fine ___ you. ___

Outro

(Instrumental)

1.

2.

Daisies

Words and Music by Katy Perry, Michael Pollack, Jon Bellion,
Jordan Johnson, Jacob Kasher Hindlin and Stefan Johnson

First note

Verse
Moderately fast

1. Told them __ your dreams and __ they all start - ed laugh - ing.
2. When did __ we all stop __ be - liev - ing __ in mag - ic?

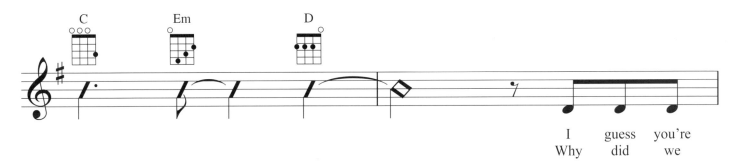

I   guess   you're
Why   did   we

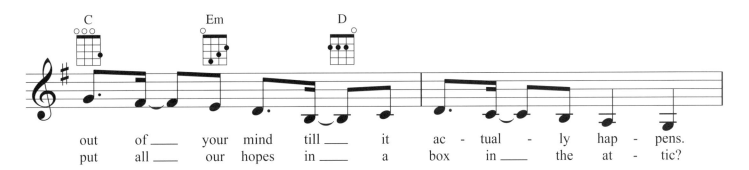

out   of __ your mind till __ it   ac - tual - ly hap - pens.
put   all __ our hopes in __ a   box in __ the   at - tic?

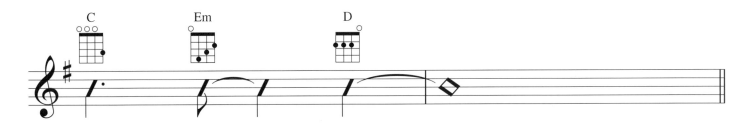

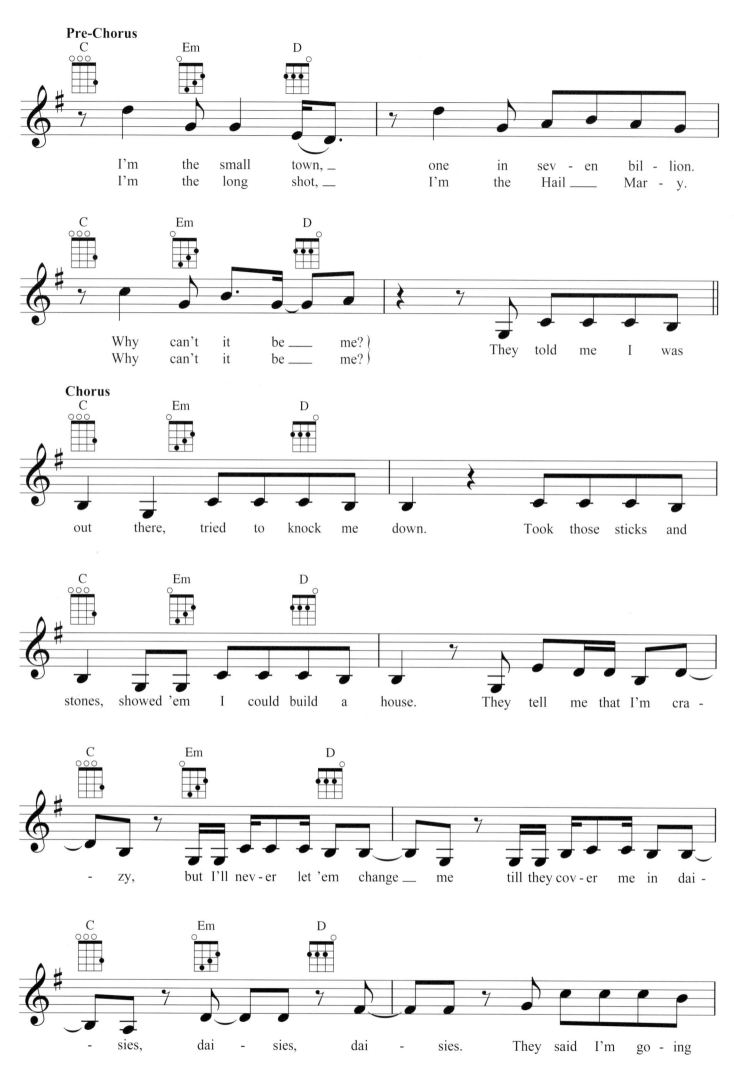

Pre-Chorus

I'm the small town, __ one in sev - en bil - lion.
I'm the long shot, __ I'm the Hail ____ Mar - y.

Why can't it be ____ me?
Why can't it be ____ me? They told me I was

Chorus

out there, tried to knock me down. Took those sticks and

stones, showed 'em I could build a house. They tell me that I'm cra -

- zy, but I'll nev - er let 'em change __ me till they cov - er me in dai -

- sies, dai - sies, dai - sies. They said I'm go - ing

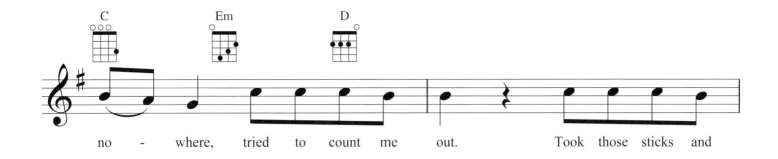

no - where, tried to count me out. Took those sticks and

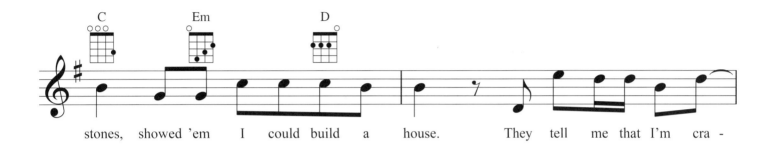

stones, showed 'em I could build a house. They tell me that I'm cra -

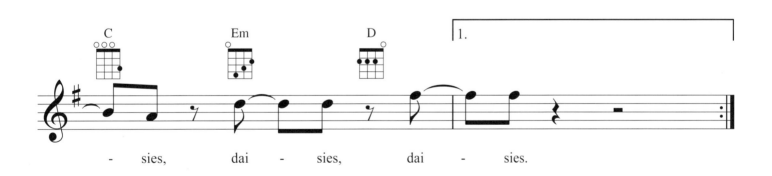

- zy, but I'll nev - er let 'em change ___ me till they cov - er me in dai -

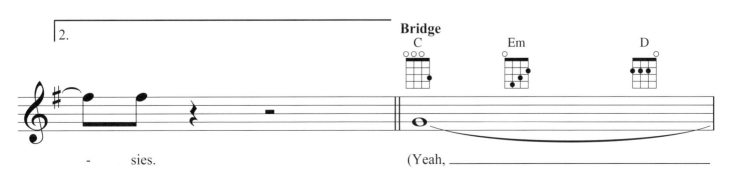

1.

- sies, dai - sies, dai - sies.

2.
                                                                    Bridge

- sies.   (Yeah, _____

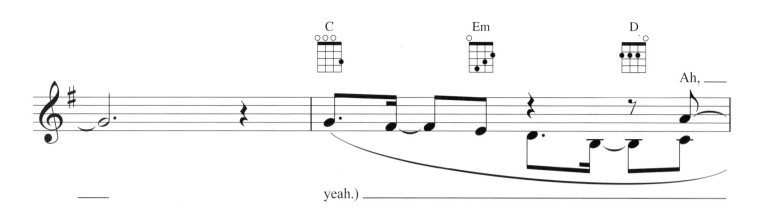

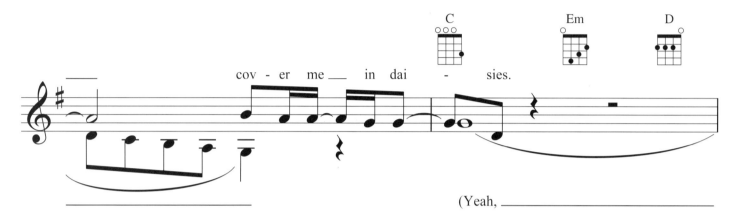

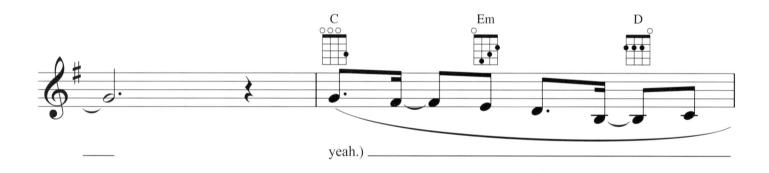

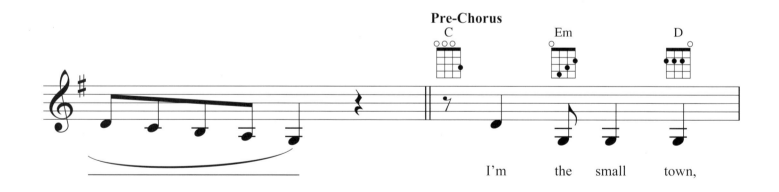

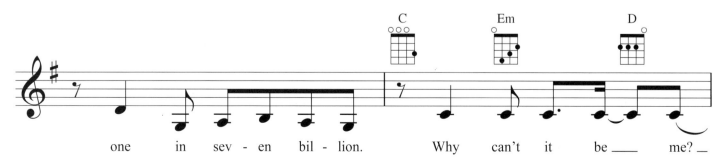

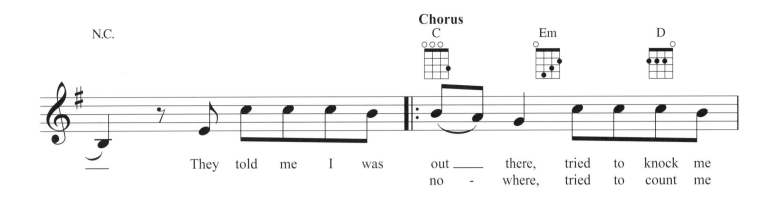

They told me I was out ___ there, tried to knock me
no - where, tried to count me

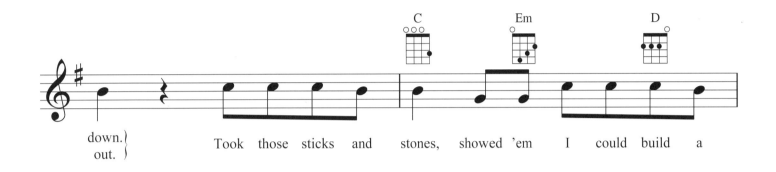

down.
out.
Took those sticks and stones, showed 'em I could build a

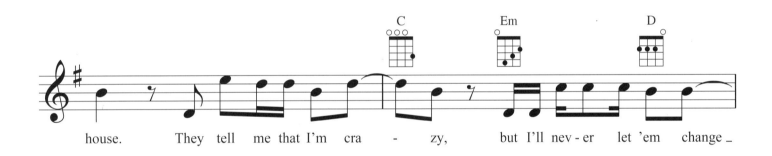

house. They tell me that I'm cra - zy, but I'll nev - er let 'em change ___

___ me till they cov - er me in dai - sies, dai - sies, dai -

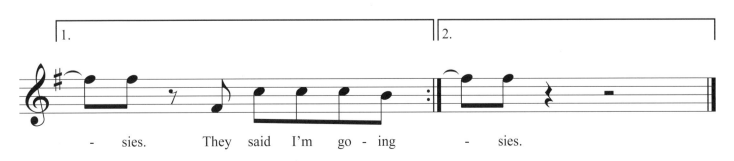

1.
- sies. They said I'm go - ing

2.
- sies.

Level of Concern

Words and Music by Tyler Joseph

First note

Verse
Moderately fast

1. Pan - ic on the brink. World __ has gone in - sane. Things __
2. Pan - ic on the brink. Mi - chael's gone in - sane. Ju -

__ are start - ing to get heav - y.
- lie starts to make you nerv - ous. I don't real - ly

I can't help but think I have - n't felt this way __ since __
care what they would say. I'm ask - ing you to stay. __ My

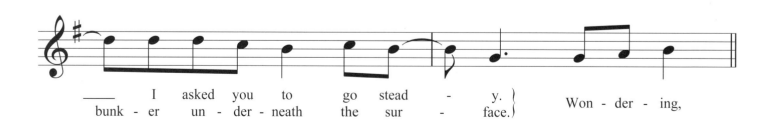

__ I asked you to go stead - y.
bunk - er un - der - neath the sur - face.} Won - der - ing,

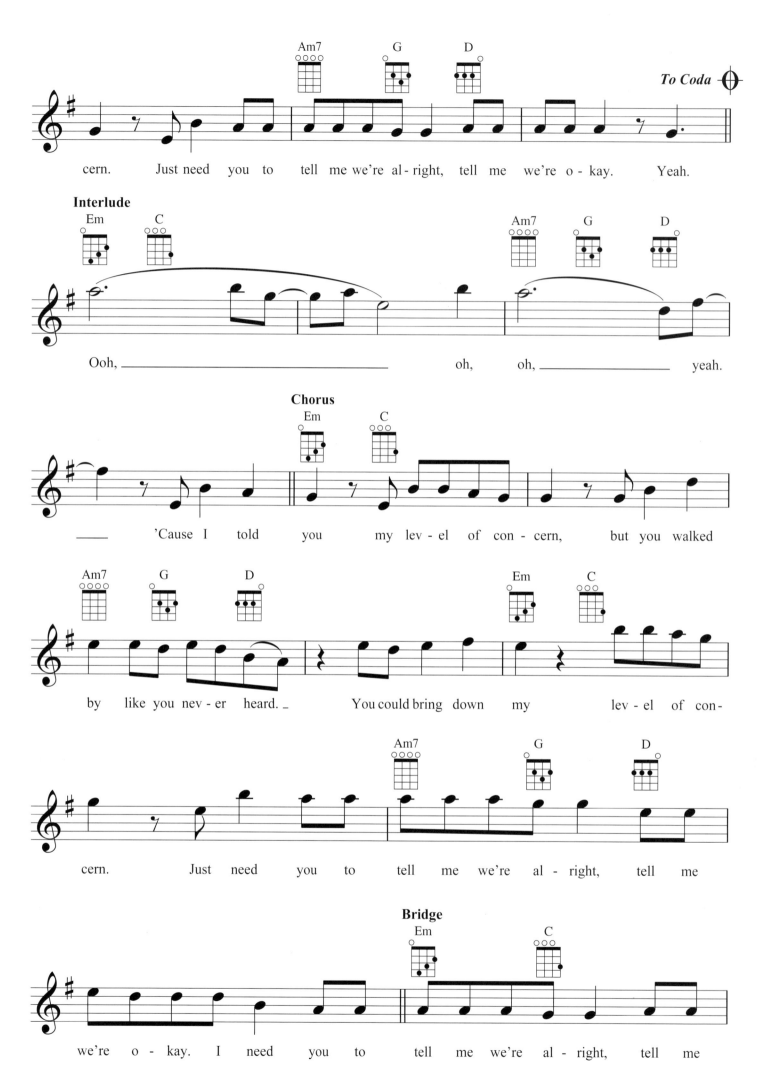

we're o - kay. Need you to tell me we're al - right, tell me

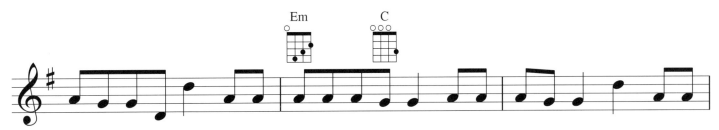

we're o - kay. I need you to tell me we're al - right, tell me we're o - kay. Need you to

Pre-Chorus 2

tell me we're al - right, tell me we're o - kay. Need you now. _____

D.S. al Coda
(take 2nd ending)

N.C.

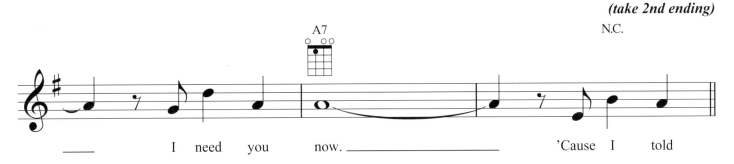

_____ I need you now. _____ 'Cause I told

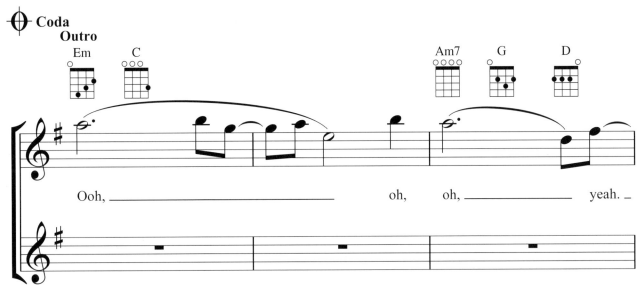

Ooh, _____ oh, oh, _____ yeah. _

(Spoken:) In a world...   ...where you can just lie to me,...   ...and I'd be okay,...

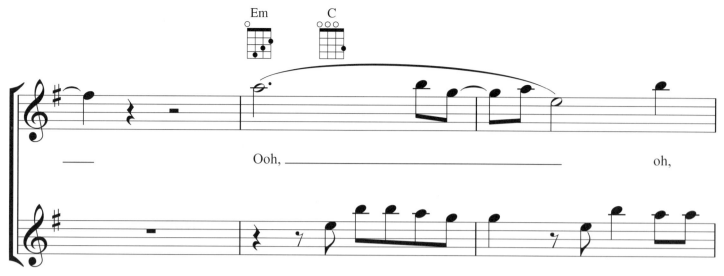

Ooh, _____ oh,

...we'll be okay.

My lev-el of con-cern.   I need you to

We're gonna be okay.

oh, _____ yeah. ___

tell me we're al - right, tell me we're o - kay. I need you.   (Need   you.

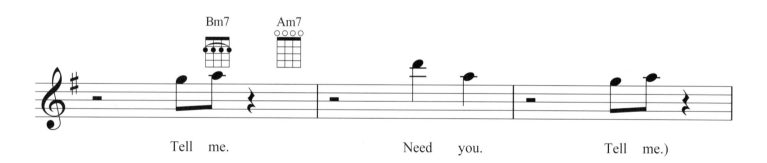

Tell me.   Need   you.   Tell me.)

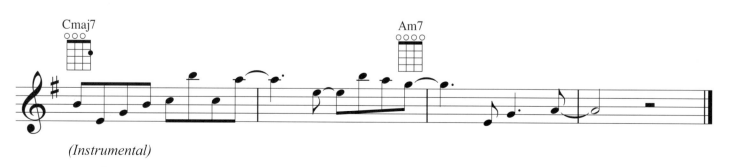

(Instrumental)

Maniac

Words and Music by Conan Gray and Daniel Nigro

First note

1. You were with your friends, par - ty - ing when the al - co - hol kicked
2. You just went too far. Wrecked your car, called me cry - ing in the

in. ____ Said you want - ed me dead. __ So, you
dark. __ Now you're break - ing my heart. __ So, I

show up at my home, all a - lone with a shov - el and a
show up at your place right a - way. Wipe the tears off of your

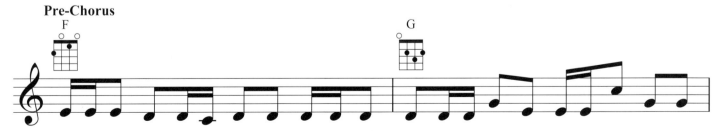

rose. __ Do you think _____ I'm a joke? __ 'Cause }
face __ while you beg _____ me to stay. __ Well, }

Pre-Chorus

peo - ple like you al - ways want back what they can't have. But I'm past that and you know that. So,

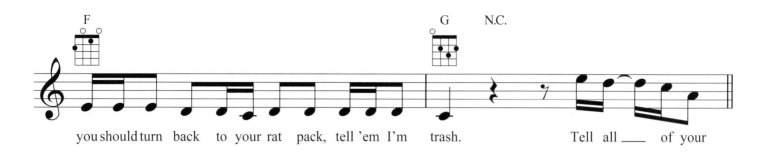

you should turn back to your rat pack, tell 'em I'm trash. Tell all __ of your

𝄋 Chorus

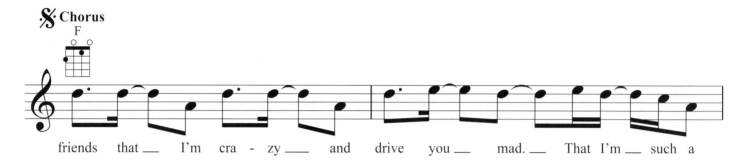

friends that __ I'm cra - zy __ and drive you __ mad. __ That I'm __ such a

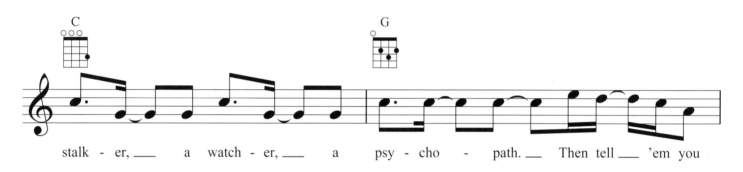

stalk - er, __ a watch - er, __ a psy - cho - path. __ Then tell __ 'em you

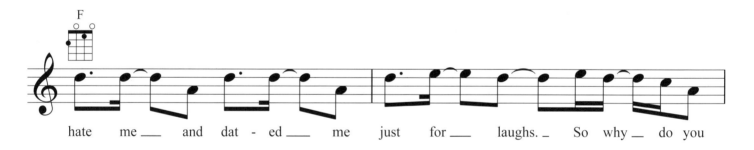

hate me __ and dat - ed __ me just for __ laughs. __ So why __ do you

call me __ and tell me __ you want me __ back? __ You ma - ni - ac.

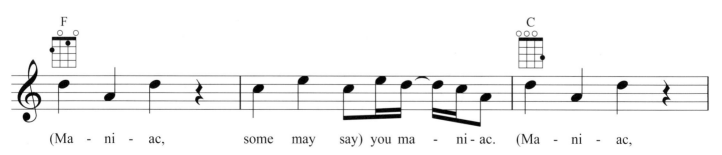

(Ma - ni - ac, some may say) you ma - ni - ac. (Ma - ni - ac,

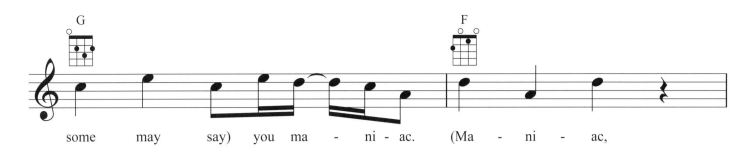

some may say) you ma - ni - ac. (Ma - ni - ac,

To Coda ⊕

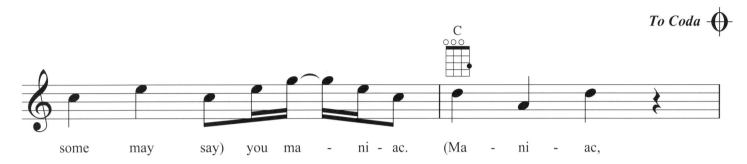

some may say) you ma - ni - ac. (Ma - ni - ac,

Bridge

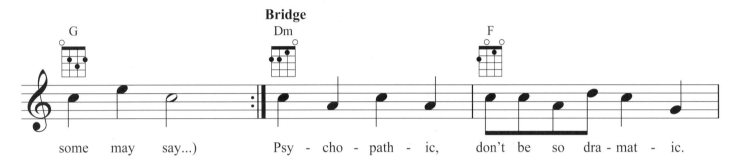

some may say...) Psy - cho - path - ic, don't be so dra - mat - ic.

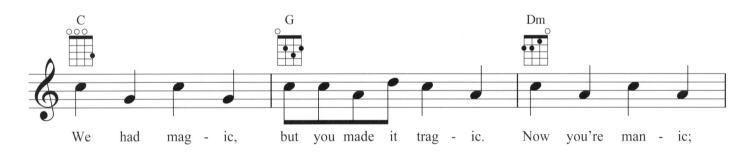

We had mag - ic, but you made it trag - ic. Now you're man - ic;

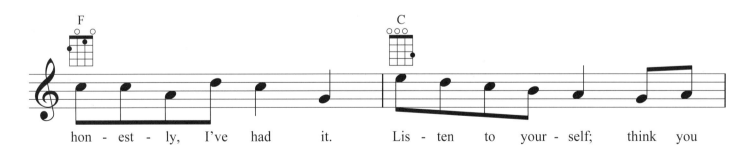

hon - est - ly, I've had it. Lis - ten to your - self; think you

⊕ **Coda**

N.C.

D.S. al Coda

need to get some help. Tell all ___ of your

some may say that I'm a....

No Time to Die

from NO TIME TO DIE

Words and Music by Billie Eilish O'Connell and Finneas O'Connell

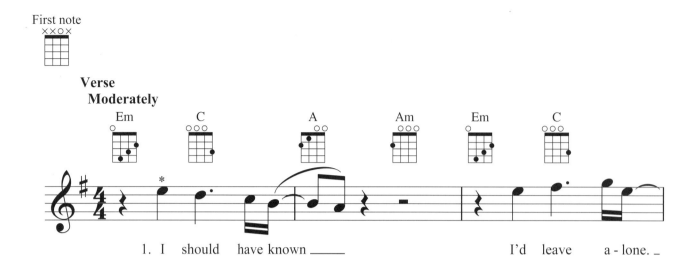

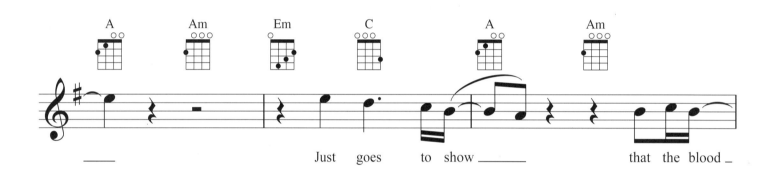

1. I should have known _____ I'd leave a - lone. _

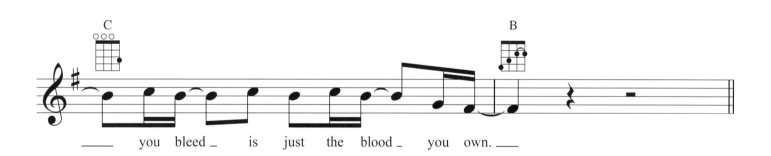

_____ Just goes to show _____ that the blood _

_____ you bleed _ is just the blood _ you own. _____

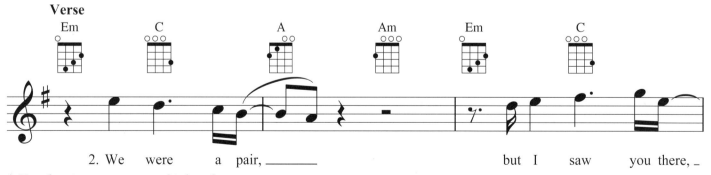

2. We were a pair, _____ but I saw you there, _

Vocal written one octave higher than sung.

_____ or par - a - dise? _ Now you'll nev - er see me cry. _

To Coda ⊕ **Interlude**

_____ There's _ just no time to die. _____

Verse

3. I let it burn _

_____ that you're no long - er my con - cern. _

_____ Fac - es from my past re - turn, _

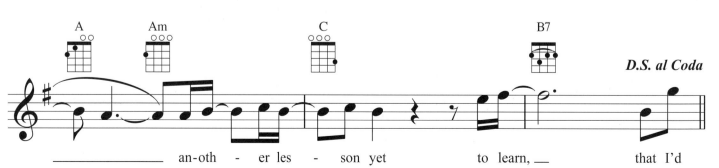

D.S. al Coda

_____ an-oth - er les - son yet to learn, _____ that I'd

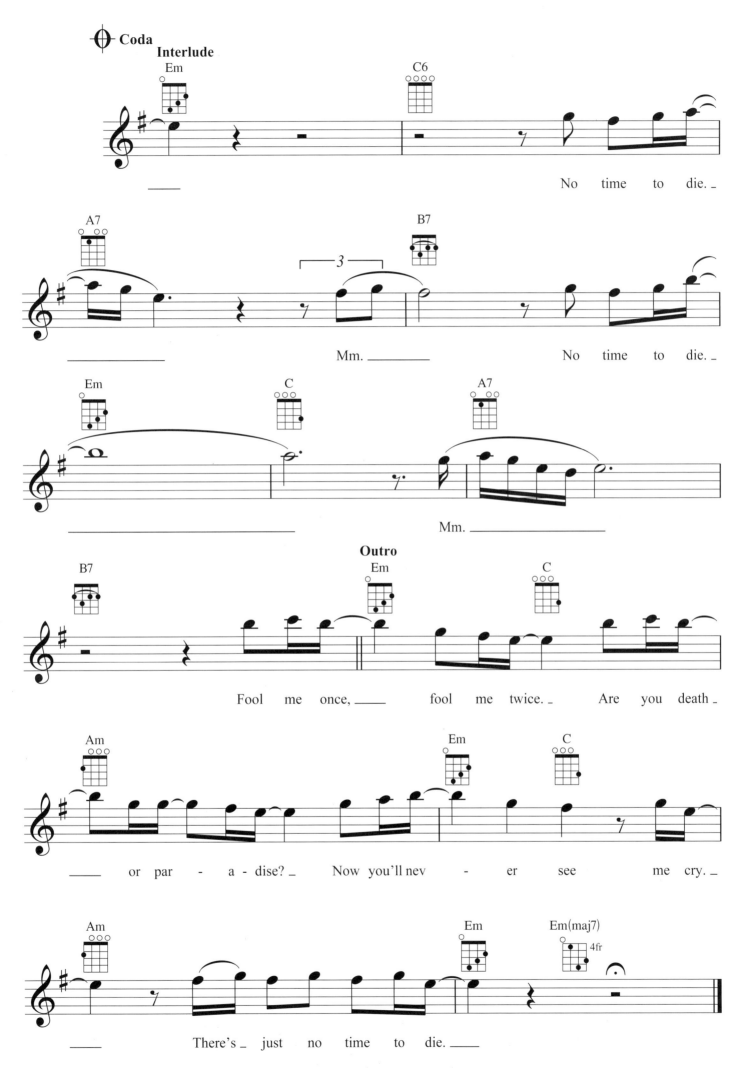

The Other Side

from TROLLS WORLD TOUR

Words and Music by Justin Timberlake, Solana Imani Rowe, Max Martin, Sarah Aarons and Ludwig Göransson

First note

Verse
Moderate Funk groove

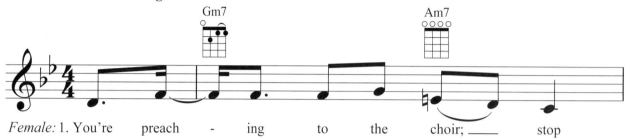

Female: 1. You're preach - ing to the choir; ___ stop

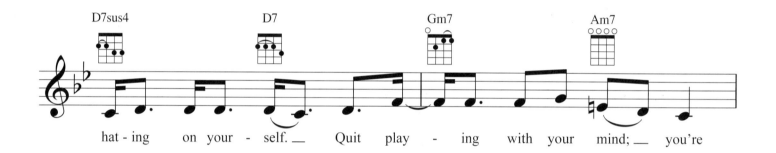

hat - ing on your - self. ___ Quit play - ing with your mind; ___ you're

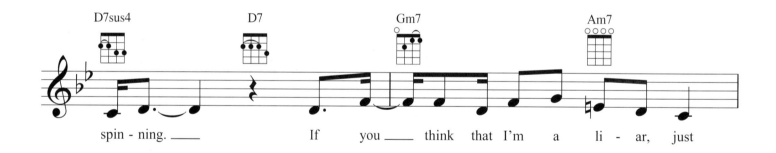

spin - ning. ___ If you ___ think that I'm a li - ar, just

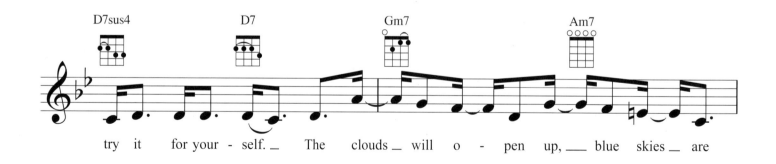

try it for your - self. ___ The clouds ___ will o - pen up, ___ blue skies ___ are

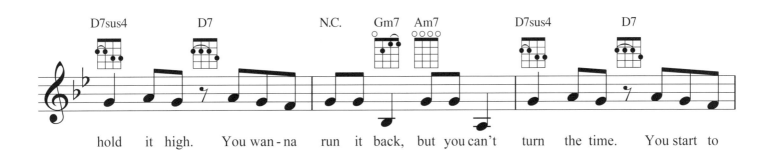

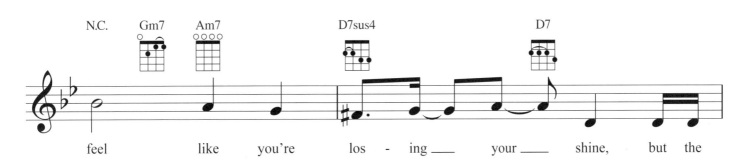

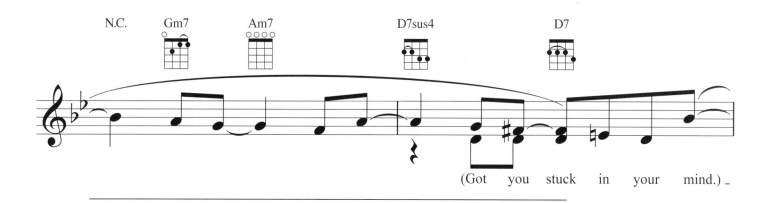

grass ain't al - ways green - er on the oth - er side. ___ (Oth - er side.) _

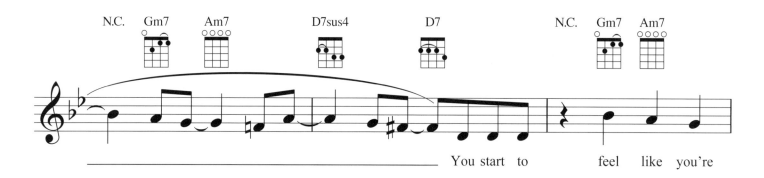

(Got you stuck in your mind.) _

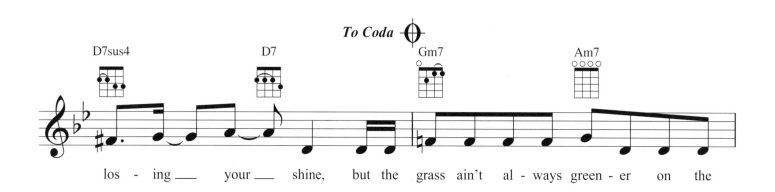

You start to feel like you're

To Coda ⊕

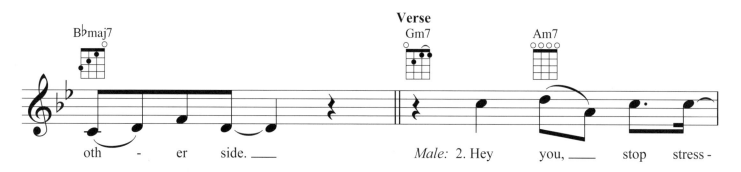

los - ing ___ your ___ shine, but the grass ain't al - ways green - er on the

Verse

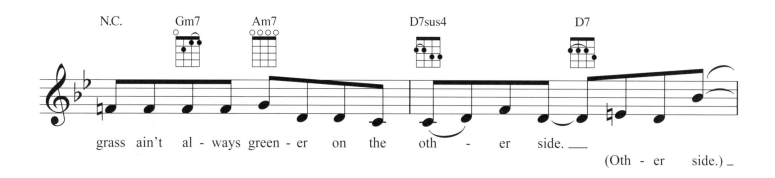

oth - er side. ___ *Male:* 2. Hey you, ___ stop stress -

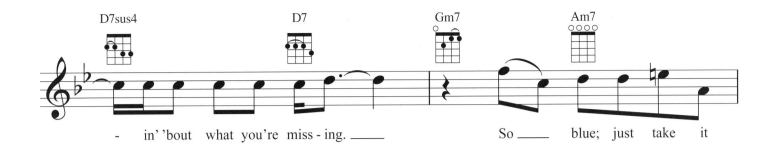

-in' 'bout what you're miss-ing. _____ So _____ blue; just take it

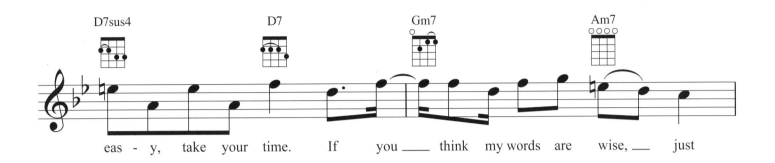

eas - y, take your time. If you _____ think my words are wise, _____ just

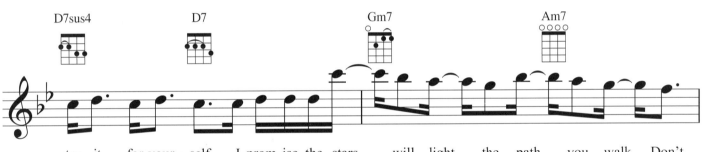

try it for your - self. I prom-ise the stars _____ will light _____ the path _____ you walk. _Don't

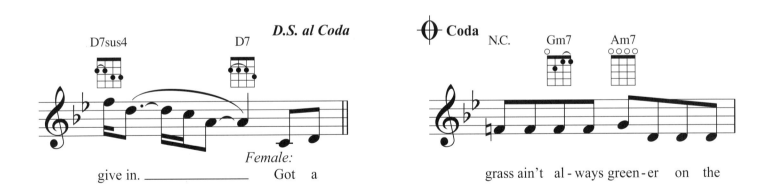

D.S. al Coda

give in. _____ *Female:* Got a

Coda

N.C.

grass ain't al - ways green - er on the

Bridge

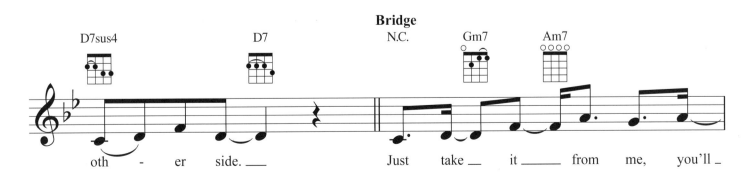

oth - er side. _____ Just take _____ it _____ from me, you'll _

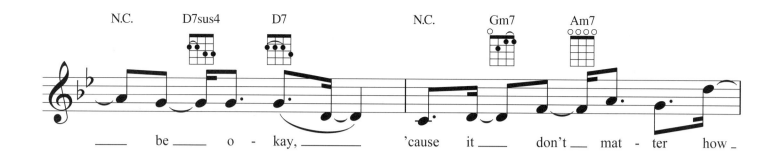

_____ be _____ o - kay, _____ 'cause it _____ don't _____ mat - ter how _

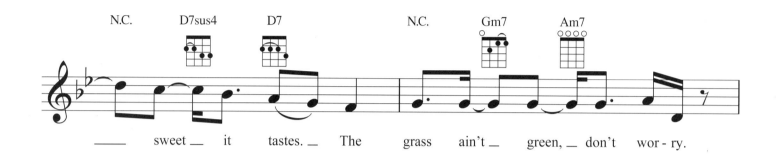

_____ sweet _____ it tastes. _____ The grass ain't _____ green, _____ don't wor - ry.

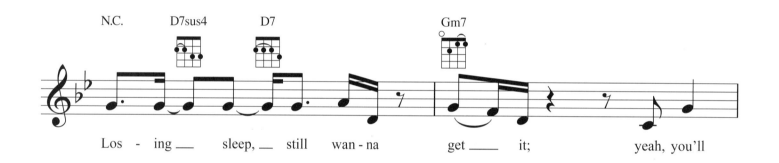

Los - ing _____ sleep, _____ still wan - na get _____ it; yeah, you'll

Chorus

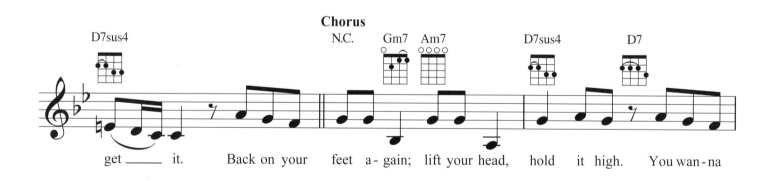

get _____ it. Back on your feet a - gain; lift your head, hold it high. You wan - na

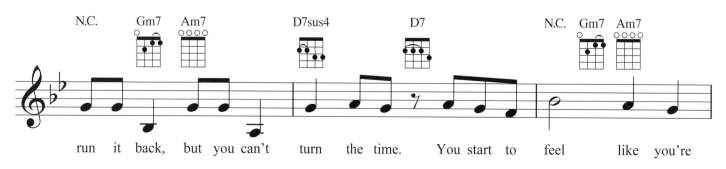

run it back, but you can't turn the time. You start to feel like you're

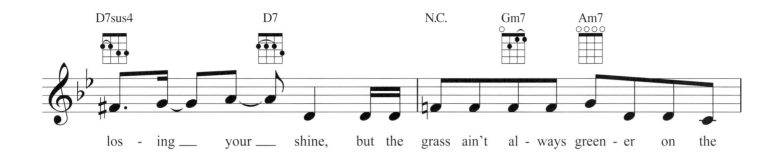

los - ing ___ your ___ shine, but the grass ain't al - ways green - er on the

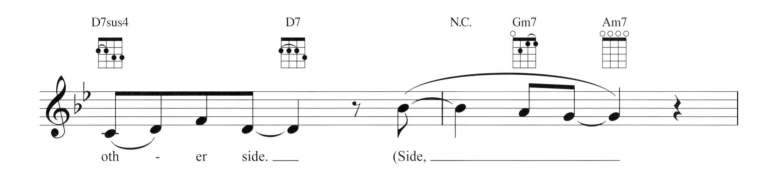

oth - er side. ___ (Side, _____

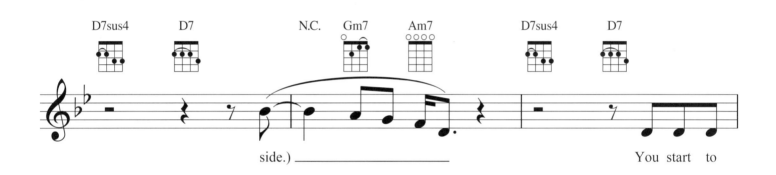

side.) _____ You start to

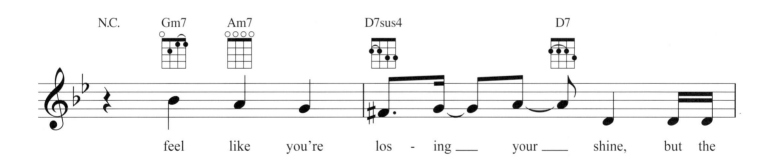

feel like you're los - ing ___ your ___ shine, but the

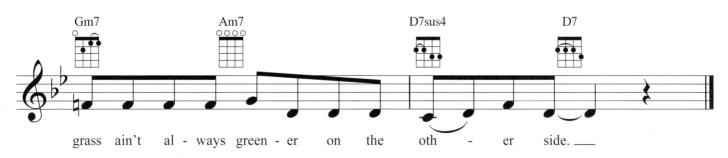

grass ain't al - ways green - er on the oth - er side. ___

Rain on Me

Words and Music by Stefani Germanotta, Martin Bresso, Michael Tucker,
Rami Yacoub, Ariana Grande, Nija Charles and Matthew Burns

First note

Verse
Upbeat Dance Pop

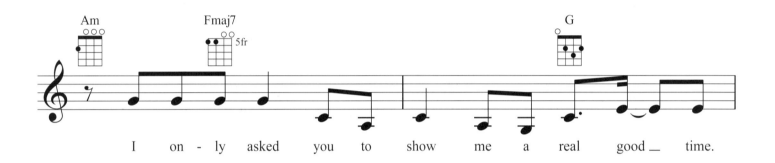

1. I did-n't ask for a free ride. ___

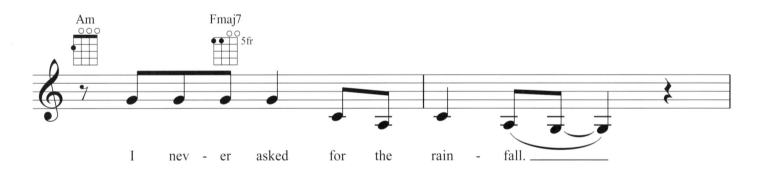

I on-ly asked you to show me a real good ___ time.

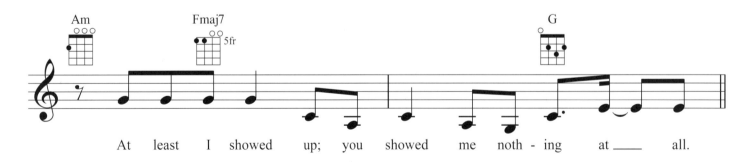

I nev-er asked for the rain-fall. ___

At least I showed up; you showed me noth-ing at ___ all.

rath - er be dry, ___ but at least I'm a - live. ___ Rain

on me, rain, rain. Rain on

Interlude

me.

To Coda ⊕

Rain on me.

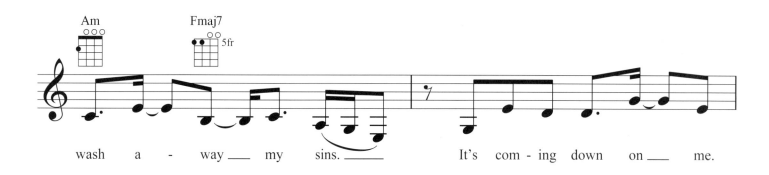

wash a - way __ my sins. _____ It's com - ing down on __ me.

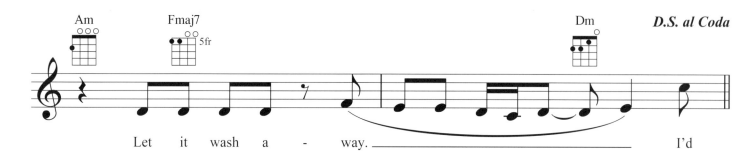

Let it wash a - way. _____ I'd

D.S. al Coda

Coda   Interlude

Rain on me.   Rain on me.

Bridge

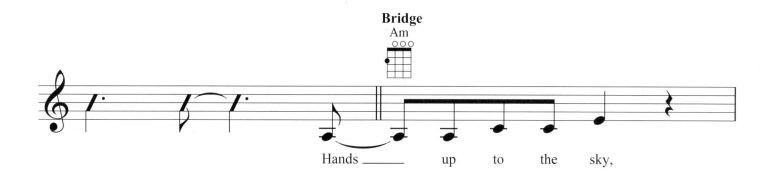

Hands _____ up to the sky,

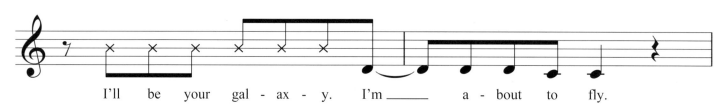

I'll be your gal - ax - y. I'm _____ a - bout to fly.

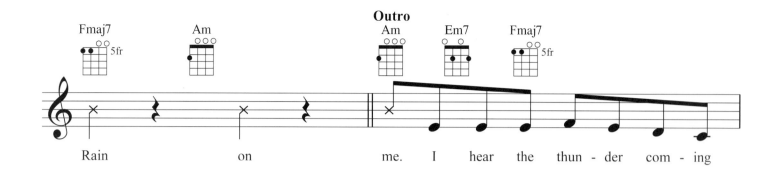

Rain   on   me.   I   hear   the   thun - der   com - ing

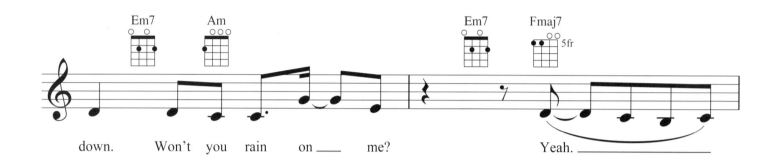

down.   Won't   you   rain   on ___ me?   Yeah. _____

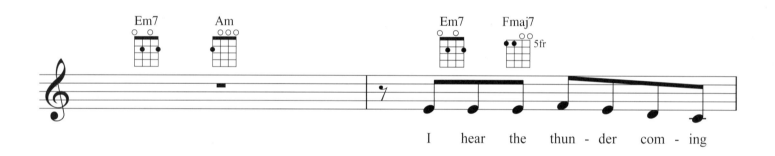

I   hear   the   thun - der   com - ing

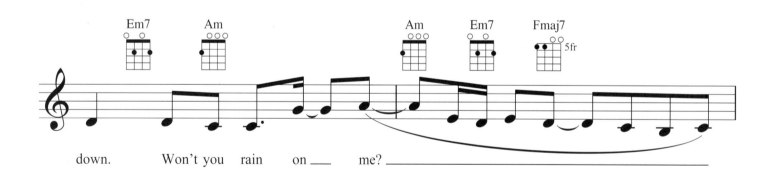

down.   Won't   you   rain   on ___ me? _____

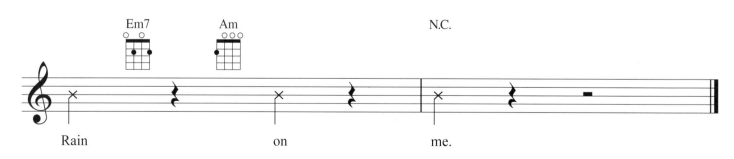

Rain   on   me.

Say So

Words and Music by Lukasz Gottwald, Amala Ratna Dlamini, Yeti Beats and Lydia Asrat

First note

Chorus
Moderately fast

Day to night to morn - ing, keep - ing me in the mo - ment. I'd

let you, had I known it. Why don't you say so? Did - n't e - ven no - tice, no

punch-es left to roll with. You got to keep me fo - cused. You want it? Say so.

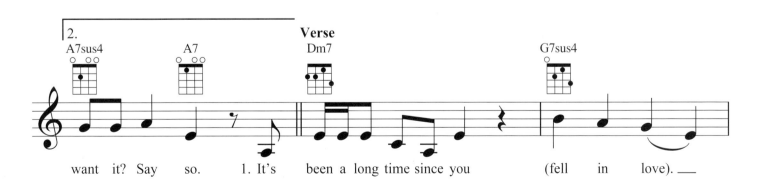

want it? Say so. 1. It's been a long time since you (fell in love). ___

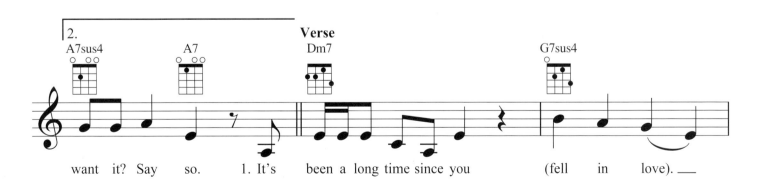

You ain't com-ing out your shell. You ain't real-ly been your-self. _____

Tell me, what must I do? (Do tell, my love.) _____ 'Cause

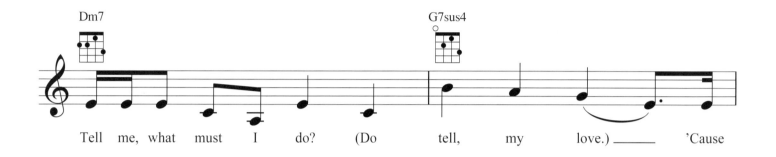

luck-i-ly I'm good at read-ing. I would-n't bug him, but he won't stop chees-ing. And

Pre-Chorus

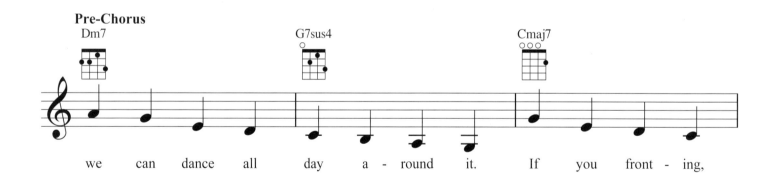

we can dance all day a-round it. If you front-ing,

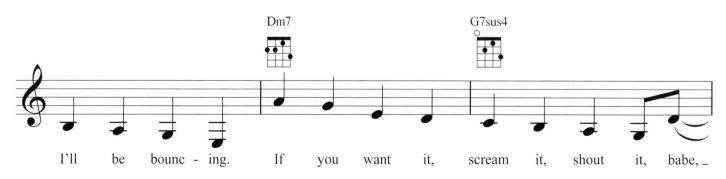

I'll be bounc-ing. If you want it, scream it, shout it, babe, _

be - fore I leave you dry. ____ Day to night to morn - ing, keep-

ing me in the mo - ment. I'd let you, had I known it. Why don't you say so?

Did-n't e - ven no - tice, no punch-es left to roll with. You got to keep me fo - cused. You

Rap

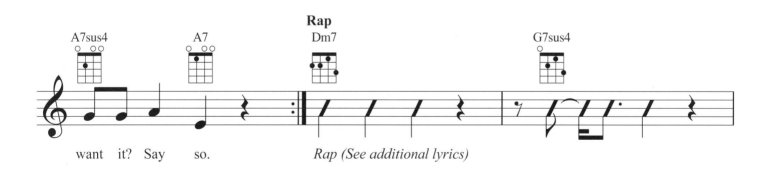

want it? Say so. *Rap (See additional lyrics)*

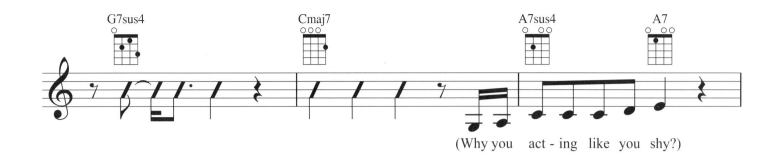

(Why you act - ing like you shy?)

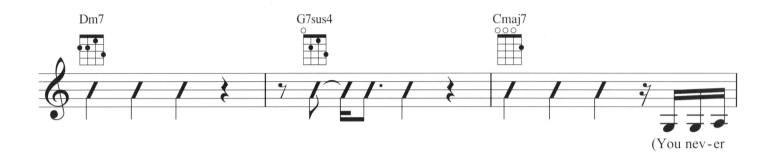

(You nev - er

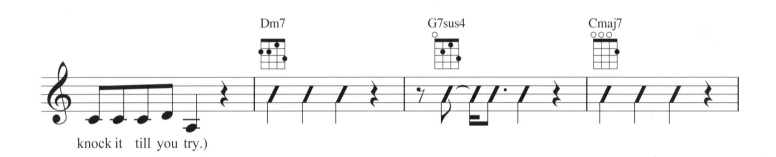

knock it till you try.)

Chorus

Day to night to morn - ing, keep - ing me in the mo - ment. I'd

let you, had I known it. Why don't you say so? Did - n't e - ven no - tice, no

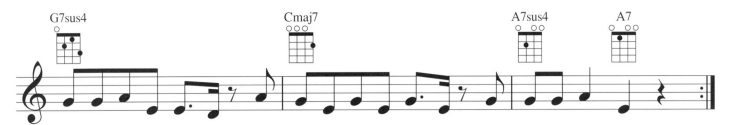

punch-es left to roll with. You got to keep me fo-cused. You want it? Say so.

Outro

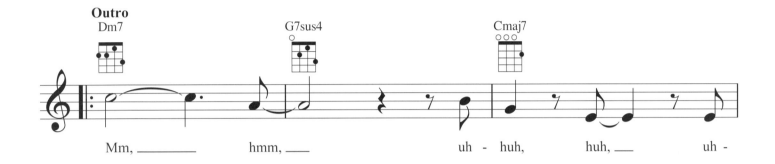

Mm, _____ hmm, ___ uh - huh, huh, ___ uh -

huh, uh - huh, uh - huh. huh, uh - huh, uh - huh.

Additional Lyrics

Rap: Let me check my chest, my breath right quick. (Ha.)
He ain't never seen it in a dress like this.
Ah, he ain't never even been impressed like this.
Prob'ly why I got him quiet on the set, like, zip.

Like it, love it, need it bad.
Take it, own it, steal it fast.
Boy, stop playing: grab my ass.

Shut it, save it, keep it pushing.
Why you beating 'round the bush,
And knowing you want all this woman?

All of them bitches hating I have you with me.
All of my niggas saying you mad committed.
Realer than anybody you had, and pretty.
All of the body-ody, the ass and titties.

Stuck with U

Words and Music by Ariana Grande, Justin Bieber, Gian Stone,
Whitney Phillips, Freddy Wexler, Skyler Stonestreet and Scooter Braun

First note

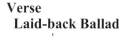

Verse
Laid-back Ballad

Female: 1. I'm not one to stick a - round.

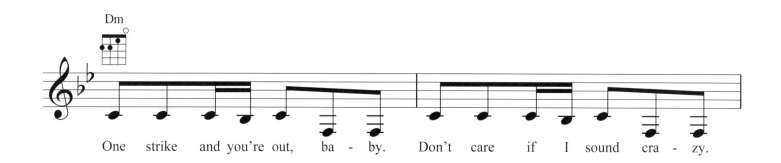

One strike and you're out, ba - by. Don't care if I sound cra - zy.

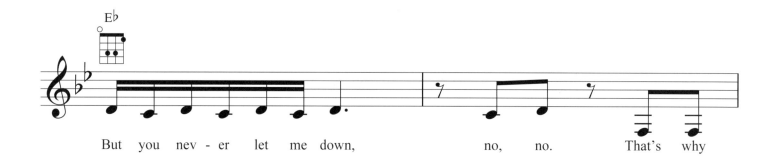

But you nev - er let me down, no, no. That's why

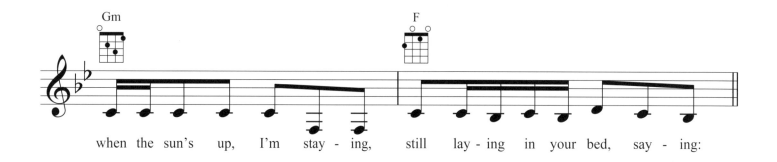

when the sun's up, I'm stay - ing, still lay - ing in your bed, say - ing:

run your mouth,   I   still would-n't change be - ing   stuck with you,   stuck with you,

To Coda

stuck with you.   I'm   stuck with you,   stuck with you,   stuck with you,   ba -

Male: 2. There's

Verse

by.   no,   no   no.
no - where we   need   to   be.

I'm - a   get   to   know   you   bet - ter,   kind - a   hope we're here   for - ev - er. There's

no - bod - y   on   these   streets. _____

If   you   told   me   that   the world's   end - ing,   ain't   no   oth - er   way   that   I   can spend   it.

Pre-Chorus

Ooh, ooh, ooh, ooh. Got all this time on — my hands. ___

Might as well can - cel ___ our plans. ___

I could stay ___ here ___ for - ev - er. So,

Coda

stuck with you. *Male:* Whoa. ___

Bridge

Ba - by, come take all my time. *Female:* Go on, make me lose my

mind. ___ *Male:* We got all that we need here to -

D.S. al Coda

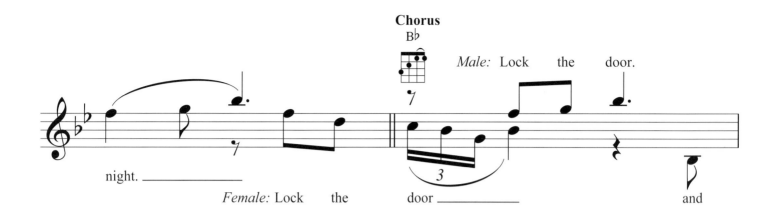

Chorus

Male: Lock the door.

night. _____

Female: Lock the door _____ and

throw out the key. Can't fight this no more,

Can't fight this no more.

it's

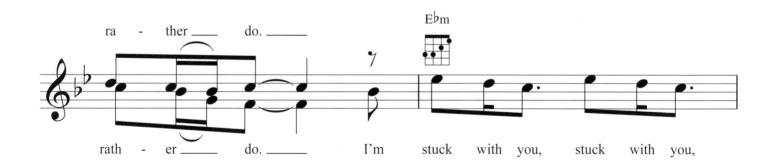

just you and me. And there's noth - ing I, noth - ing I'd

Noth - ing I'd

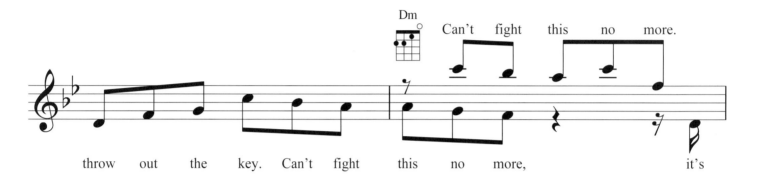

ra - ther ___ do. _____

rath - er ___ do. _____ I'm stuck with you, stuck with you,

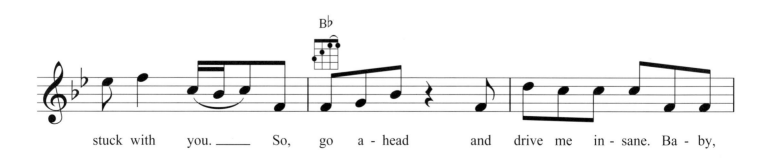

stuck with you. ___ So, go a - head and drive me in - sane. Ba - by,

run your mouth,   I   still would-n't change all   this   lov-ing you,   hat-ing you,

want - ing you.   I'm   stuck with you,   stuck with you,   stuck with ____

Outro

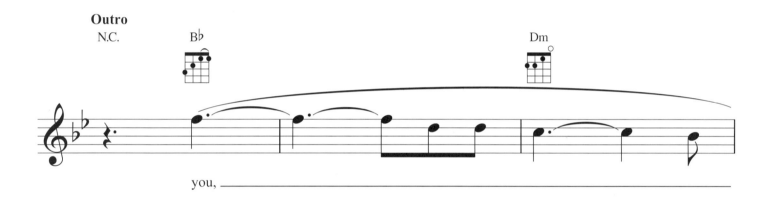

you, _____

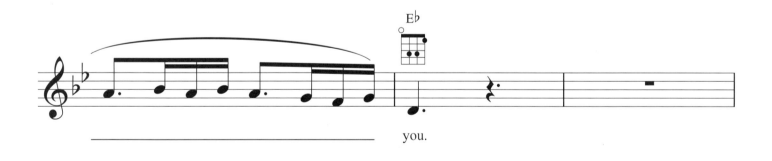

_____ you.

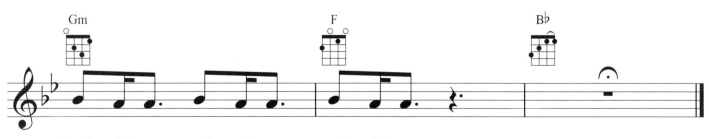

Stuck with you,   stuck with you,   stuck with you.

What a Man Gotta Do

Words and Music by Nick Jonas, Joseph Jonas, Kevin Jonas, Ryan Tedder, Jessica Agombar and David Stewart

First note

Verse
Energetic Pop Rock

C5

1. Caught my heart ___ a - bout one, two times, don't
2. You ain't tryin' ___ to be wast - ing time on

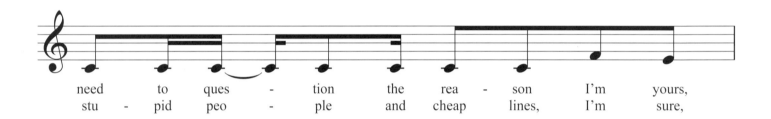

need to ques - tion the rea - son I'm yours,
stu - pid peo - ple and cheap lines, I'm sure,

I'm yours. _____ I'd
I'm sure. _____ So, I'd

F

move the earth ___ or lose a fight just to see ___ you smile 'cause you got no flaws,
give a mil - lion dol - lars just for you to grab ___ me by the col - lar and I'll come build us,

no flaws. _____ ⎫
build us. _____ ⎭   I'm not

Pre-Chorus

tryin' to be ___ your part - time lov - er.   Sign me up ___ for that full - time, I'm yours,

I'm yours. _____   So, what a man got - ta

𝄋 Chorus

do?   What a man got - ta   do _____   to be

to - tal - ly ___ locked up by you?   What a man got - ta

say?   What a man got - ta   pray _____   to be your

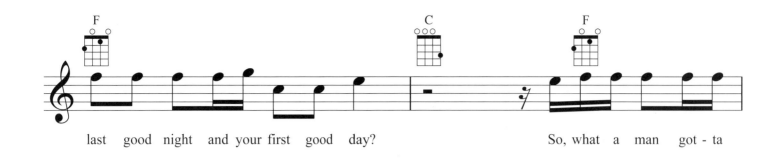

last   good   night   and   your   first   good   day?   So,   what   a   man   got - ta

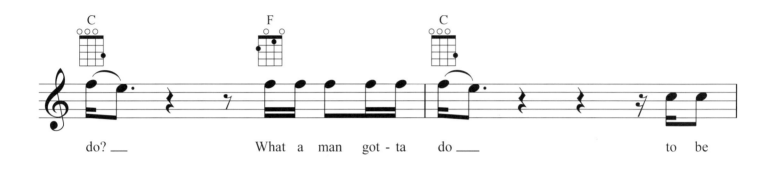

do? __   What   a   man   got - ta   do __   to   be

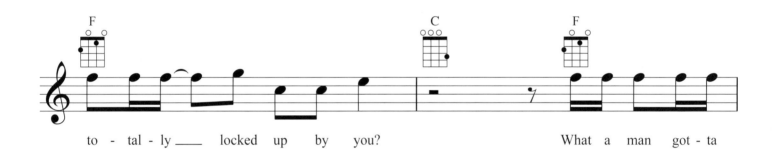

to - tal - ly __   locked   up   by   you?   What   a   man   got - ta

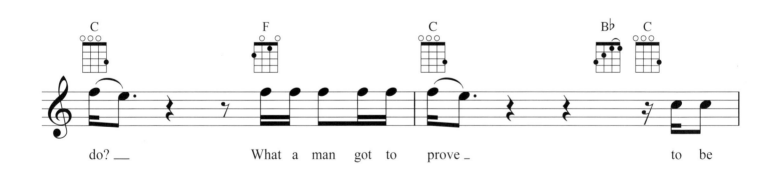

do? __   What   a   man   got   to   prove _   to   be

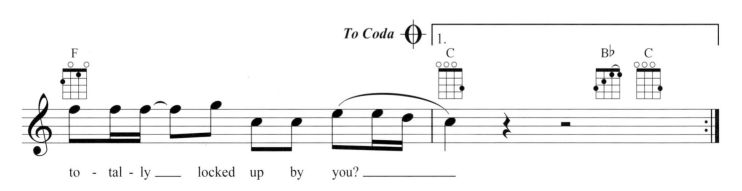

to - tal - ly __   locked   up   by   you? _____

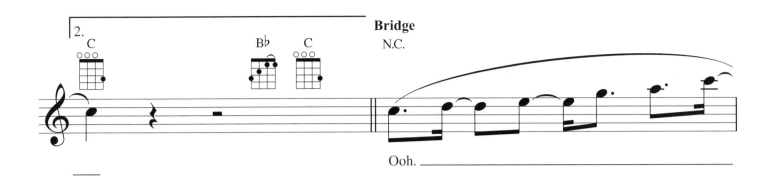

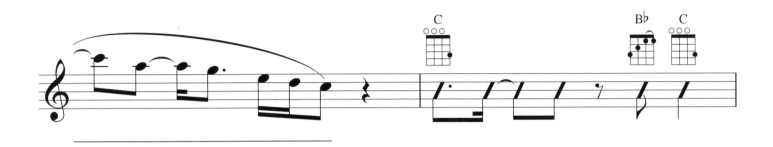

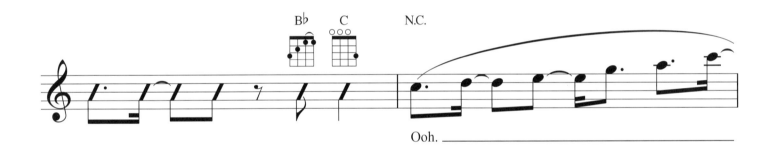

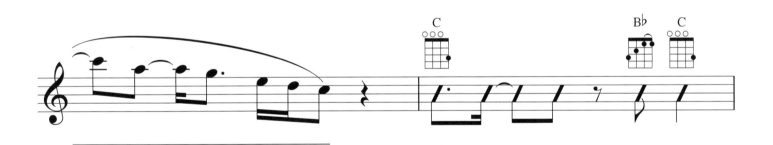

Tell me what a man ___ got - ta
So, what a man got - ta

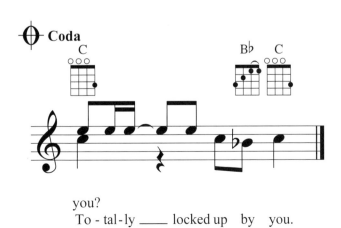

you?
To - tal - ly ___ locked up by you.

Sunday Best

Words and Music by Forrest Frank and Colin Padalecki

First note

Chorus
Moderately

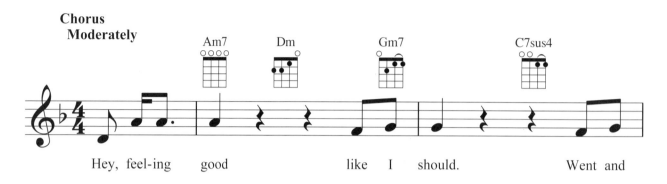

Hey, feel-ing good like I should. Went and

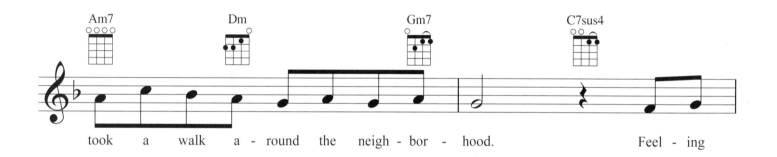

took a walk a - round the neigh - bor - hood. Feel - ing

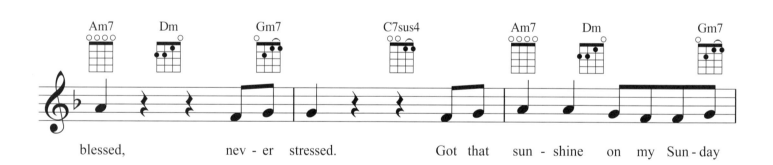

blessed, nev - er stressed. Got that sun - shine on my Sun - day

Verse

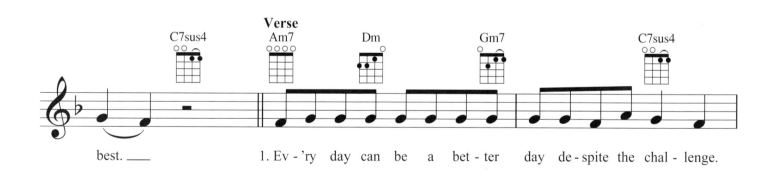

best. ___ 1. Ev - 'ry day can be a bet - ter day de - spite the chal - lenge.

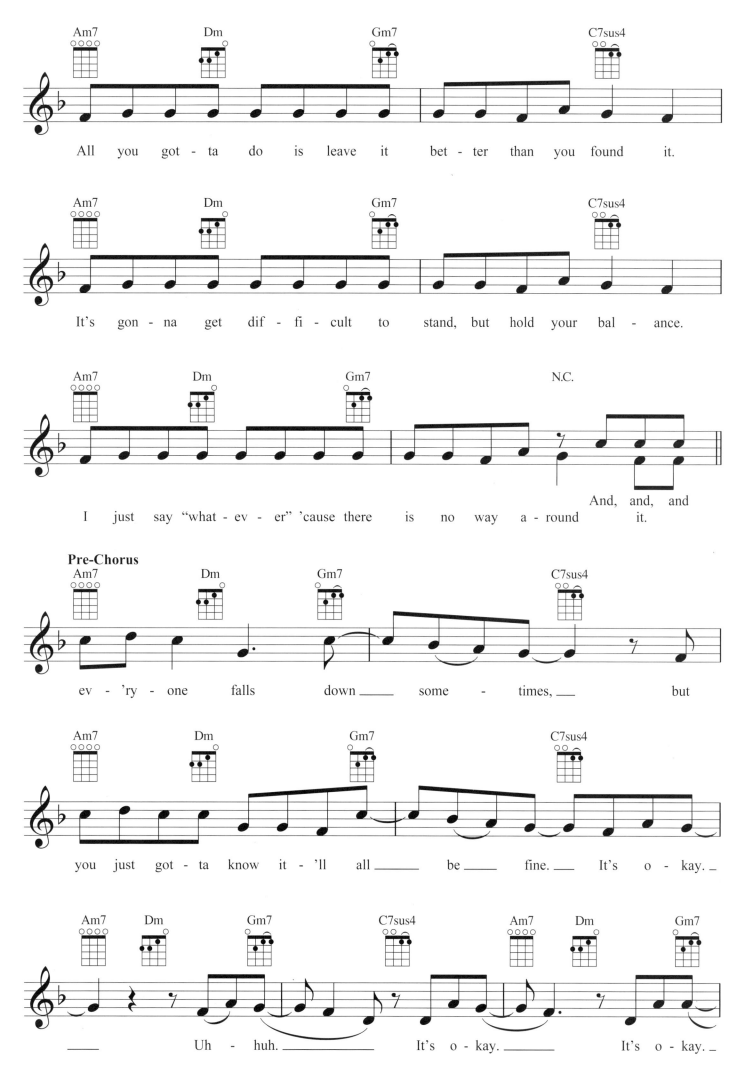

All you got - ta do is leave it bet - ter than you found it.

It's gon - na get dif - fi - cult to stand, but hold your bal - ance.

I just say "what - ev - er" 'cause there is no way a - round it.

And, and, and

Pre-Chorus

ev - 'ry - one falls down _____ some - times, _____ but

you just got - ta know it - 'll all _____ be _____ fine. _____ It's o - kay. _

_____ Uh - huh. _____ It's o - kay. _____ It's o - kay. _

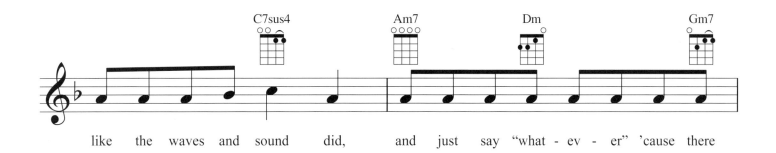

like the waves and sound did, and just say "what - ev - er" 'cause there

Pre-Chorus

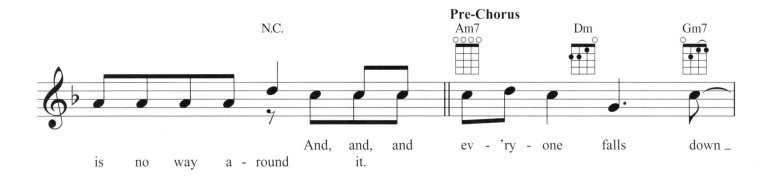

And, and, and ev - 'ry - one falls down ___

is no way a - round it.

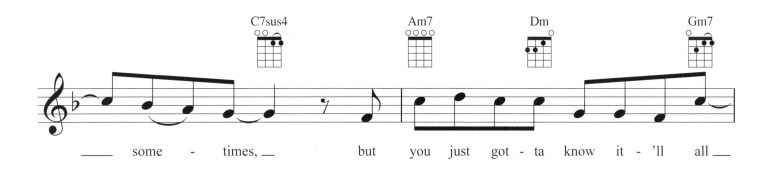

___ some - times, ___ but you just got - ta know it - 'll all ___

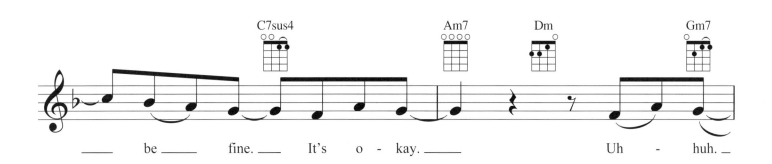

___ be ___ fine. ___ It's o - kay. ___ Uh - huh. ___

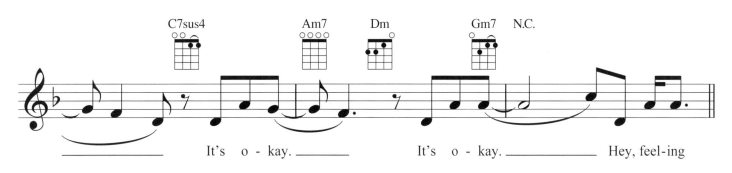

_____ It's o - kay. ___ It's o - kay. _____ Hey, feel - ing

Chorus

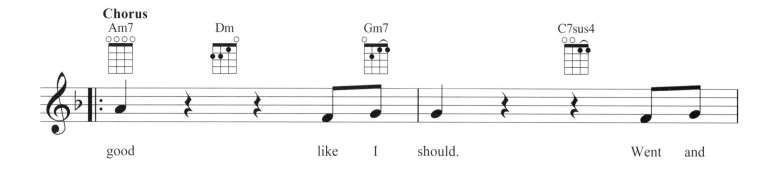

good   like   I   should.   Went   and

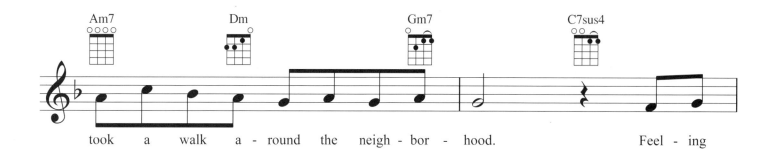

took   a   walk   a - round   the   neigh - bor - hood.   Feel - ing

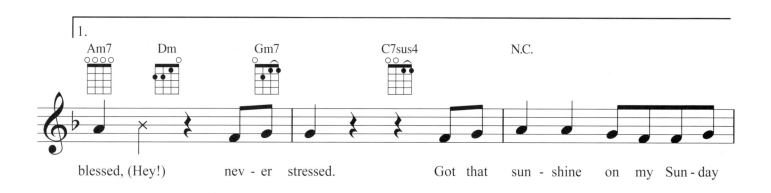

blessed, (Hey!)   nev - er   stressed.   Got   that   sun - shine   on   my   Sun - day

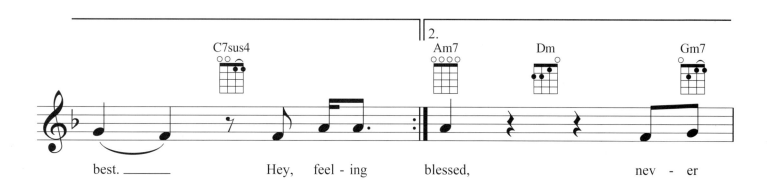

best. _____   Hey,   feel - ing   blessed,   nev - er

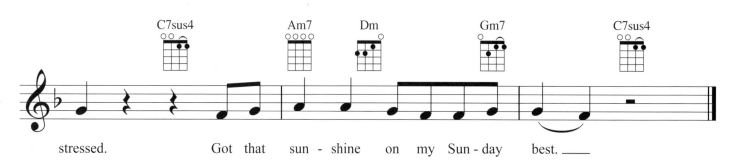

stressed.   Got   that   sun - shine   on   my   Sun - day   best. ____